LIVE BY YOUR OWN RULES!

GISELA DI FABIO

LIVE BY YOUR OWN RULES!

BREAK FREE FROM SOCIAL AND FAMILY MANDATES

Cover Design: Valentina Lava

Editing: Andrae D. Smith, Jr.

Haydée Asunta and José.
My parents.
For their unconditional love and encouragement, and because I've always been perfect for them just as I am.

CONTENTS

I

"READY, SET, GO!"

1

WHY NOW?

If not now, then when?

"I refuse to believe that this will be my life forever. Eventually, I will leave this job and follow my passion."

I've heard and thought that so many times! If you have too, then welcome to the club!

You may have noticed there are many kinds of people in the world. I like to divide them into two groups:

(1) Those who have dreams and ask themselves, "What if…?" or "How did I end up living this life?" "What am I doing with my life?" or even "Is my life always going to be like this?"

(2) Those who are thriving and have their dream lives.

I can also divide the first group. There are those who wonder, "How can I make my life different?" "How can I get where I want to be?"—the curious group. These are the people who may be considered "reckless" for choosing to take action and crossing through the door that just opened in front of them. They don't let any circumstance define them, they own their story and they know that their actions will make the difference and define them. The warriors.

And of course, the other group is made of those who will tell themselves they will follow their dreams "one day." Those people lie to themselves with excuses and justify themselves to avoid acting. The group that are imprisoned by their circumstances. The victims of their fate.

This book is for the group that asks the questions, and are ready to find an answer. If you are part of the "victim" group and you are still not ready to move to the "warrior" group, then, you can leave the book and come back when you are ready. I hope you get ready soon, life is too short to play small!

Warriors, welcome! I'm happy to be writing these pages for you because I am in that group too. We are kindred spirits.

I have had a great life. I consider myself privileged for many reasons, from the fact that I was born in my family and being loved, cared for, and respected, to having access to education and many other opportunities. Life has given me a lot, and I've always been committed to making the best out of it. I've always felt it was my responsibility, that I owed it to God, in the sense of gratitude. This responsibility has to do with helping others, and honoring my life through making choices.

Although I've always felt grateful, I consistently felt that there was something more. I used to feel stressed, burnt out, overwhelmed, desperate, wondering what the purpose of all my work and energy was. Where was it going?. It was a misinterpretation of that responsibility that I felt I had, instead of enjoying my life and choosing how to live, I was living through expectations and mandates. I suffered from frequent migraines, stomachaches, anxiety, and other stress-related symptoms as my body tried to tell me that something was wrong.

Back then, I only had those questions. Wonders and

curiosity, but no answers. I didn't know exactly where I was supposed to go, I just knew that there was something more, that there was a key that I wasn't finding to open the door to the other side, the side where life was extremely colorful. (If you haven't seen *Trolls* (2016) yet, you need to watch it! That's how a colorful life looks like for me.) In reality, I was craving freedom. I felt held back, like a force was preventing me from getting where I was meant to be, and I had no idea what to do.

My dream was simple: "I want to do what I want to, when I want to and how I want to!" When I read it now, it's so clear for me that the only hold back was myself. I was the one preventing me from reaching my full potential. Yes, you read that right. I was standing in my own way. The truth is, despite all my blessings, I was still a part of the "victims" group. I used to justify myself, making excuses that made it impossible to break myself free from family and social mandates to live that dream.

Now I know this dream is not only possible. My journey has made it possible. I learned through my experience that getting to this point in my life needed many difficult and impactful decisions (some of them, I will tell you about in this book), and that each of them is worth it.

I never thought that, at thirty-three years old, I would be working passionately in my purpose, feeling free, and having this understanding of "happiness." I didn't think that "happiness" would look like the life I have right now. I never thought I would have started a new career at thirty, that would become my full-time job later. I never thought I would be here writing this book. Specifically, I never thought I would be recently separated, that I wouldn't have kids, among other life events. But this is one of the best learning experiences, we are not expectations, mandates, or plans, life will happen, and the sooner we take responsibility for the decisions that we can make, the better, because most times we don't have the opportunity to choose the events, and in those moments, how we go through those events is what defines us.

If you asked me "what would I tell my twenty-three-year-old version?" I would say that I see her and that she is enough. I would also say that she doesn't have to be scared and she needs to trust she will be fine. God and the universe have a plan for each of us. The great thing about now is that I don't need my forty-three-year-old version to tell me that I will be fine. I lived enough to know that life won't throw at us any event that we are not ready to overcome. That for every challenge that we face, there will be tools and resources to navigate them in the best way. That life has highs and lows, and in the low parts is when miracles happen, and that leaving those lows depends on us. That it doesn't matter how many plans we have, what matters is to learn how to adapt to life events, because those turns will happen anyway, and if we want to avoid going through the same issue or difficulty over and over again, we need to figure out the lesson that life is trying to teach us. If you believe you can, you will certainly make it happen.

My editor told me that life gives us the tests before we face the next challenge. This means that I was ready to write the book before I acknowledged that I was ready.

It's crazy how many times I wondered and asked myself if I was ready. And how I knew in my heart that I've always been.

Why now?

It is now because I'm truly committed to myself and all those younger versions of myself that are going through life wondering, just wondering what else is out there for me? For all those people that know in their hearts that they are meant for something different. For each and every person that gets up every morning and when they look in the mirror don't recognize themselves. For those who are living a life that is not even close to what they expected their life would be. For all the unique people that don't fit in the standards.

Why now?

Because you and I know that you are ready to make it happen, and when you take your first step, don't thank me, thank yourself, because nobody can do the work for you. If you are ready to start a journey that will take your life to the next level, then keep on reading. If it doesn't sound like you, don't worry, I came to the acknowledgement that not everything is for everyone, and not everyone likes everything, uniqueness is exactly like that. I am confident that if this book is meant to be for you, it will find a way back to you when it is the right time.

I wish you a life full of brave decisions, happy choices, and purposefulness!

Why now?

Because I am tired of being uncomfortable, I decided to put my opinion, perspective, and feelings out there. I am doing it from love, vulnerability, and an open heart. Nothing in this book is *the* method; however it is mine. Nothing in this book is *the* perspective, it is just mine.

After having the opportunity to share my opinions, perspectives, and methods with different people, and finding that it was useful, I am doing it through this book with the hope that more people will find it useful and comforting, that it will help them learn and change their perspective.

Why now?

Because your future starts today, and the time is perfect. Make it happen!

JOURNAL IT

2

WHAT BROUGHT ME HERE

I LOVE RULES, and I follow them. I also have policies that I create for myself, and I try to stick to them. They keep my structure, I consider them efficient because they are a shortcut to making some decisions, they give me a feeling of being more organized and under control.

The problem with rules is that sometimes they are limiting.

We all heard that rules were made to be broken. That's not my favorite phrase, I have encountered feelings with that statement. On one hand, rules end up being limiting, and on the other hand, they can be useful. So I wonder, how can I find a balance?

On the third hand, I was obviously obsessed with doing the right thing—doing what I must and doing it well. Yes, it's a lot, have you ever felt that you have a personal assistant inside your head whose only function is to be hard on you and create doubts? Well, I have one of those!

As for finding the balance, I don't have the answer for that question, but what I can say is that I used to follow all the rules, social rules, family rules, friends' rules, couples' rules, and they started to build up in my head, until I disconnected my mind from my body. I got to a point where I stopped caring about what I wanted, and I only cared about rules, expectations, and mandates.

I am Gisela, I am a person.

I was born and raised in Buenos Aires, Argentina. I've been living in Miami since 2015, and I would like to share part of my background with you.

I come from a Greek-Italian family. I have two brothers and two sisters. I am the second child, the first girl. My parents always loved me unconditionally just as I am. However, some family members loved me as they knew, through their expectations, their experience and through their limitations.

I grew up doing everything I was supposed to, I went to school, I've never had great test results but I've always behaved. I went to university and got my degree in business administration at twenty-three. As I said, I grew up checking the "musts" list. By that time, I was already working with my father, and as soon as I got my degree, I became the General Manager of one of the family businesses. My father became my mentor, that was another opportunity that my parents gave me. Both made the decision, while in the practice I was working directly with my father. An opportunity that shaped my career and me as a professional, I will always be grateful for.

I worked hard, performed well, and achieved results. After some time, I started to study again. I was having a balanced life, the only thing I didn't have was a partner, and somehow it always seemed to be the most important thing to have.

I grew up hearing that I was "ready to get married" when something I cooked was good. And when I went back to the university, I was questioned, "Why would you keep on studying? Find a boyfriend!" When I would get frustrated, I was told, "with that temper you won't find a boyfriend!" or "Your standards are too high! You need to lower your expectations!" I've always fought to find my place, to make sure that my voice was heard, yet for a long time, in my family, my worth was reduced to the fact that I didn't have a boyfriend.

When I eventually realized how those phrases had shaped some of my behaviors, I started to feel angry with those people that used to say those things to me and to other women. But my therapist, Justo, explained to me that it wasn't their fault. People see the world as they believe it is, through their own experience and filters. We all say things, and the impact of those things have to do with us, with our personality. So there are no blames, there are just different perspectives and personalities that absorb more of those ideas. This acknowledgement is part of what brought me here, because none of those people said those things on purpose, still those ideas shaped my behavior. The reason I'm putting myself out there now, is so we can all pay more attention to the ideas in our minds, gain some perspective, and make sure that we do things on purpose. And also, for all those people that, like me, shaped their behavior according to those expressions, so they have the opportunity to deconstruct and build those ideas again, and break free, as I did.

As a young female professional, I was also underestimated. I adapted to belong to a profession where most of my peers were men. Overworked and determined to prove that I could get things done, I became an overachiever to make sure I got recognition. But it was never enough to fulfill me. Who was I trying to really impress? What was I trying to prove? I used to spend so much time trying to belong, I was living with the constant feeling that I was not normal, I didn't belong anywhere, (except with my closest friends). I used to pretend, and by doing that I was denying my true self. If you're reading this book, maybe you've been here too. Maybe you've had that same feeling of not fitting perfectly, of apologizing too much, thinking too much about what others may think about you. Maybe you've felt anxiety about something that happened that triggered your insecurities, and then, the non-stop thought of guilt about that single moment when you did something that was not representing you. I want you to know that you're not alone. I've been there. I see you.

At twenty-seven, I moved to Miami with my sister, Fiorella. We bought a franchise and opened a business. We worked so hard that it is even hard to remember those days. Our family visited us on a regular basis, so even though we had difficulties at work, we were receiving a lot of support and encouragement. We were still pretty stressed about the business. I was frustrated, tired and miserable. We were making progress but it was slow and extremely demanding.

As soon as I found some free time during the week I started to study Coaching at the University of Miami. It lasted almost one year. Through coaching I met Andrew, who a year later became my husband. Our relationship gave me many moments that I will cherish forever. Being together helped me to face many challenges, and make difficult decisions. I learned a lot about myself, about relationships, and about many other things. I will be forever grateful for that relationship. Our wedding was the last time that my family got together for a celebration. By that moment my mother already had been diagnosed with cancer.

She passed away in February 2020, and we were all devastated. There are no words for that moment. All I can say is that the impact changed something in me, part of me was transformed with her transformation.

A couple of months after that I left my company. According to the agreement that I had with my sister, I sold my part to her. I felt that that business took so many moments from me that I couldn't bear to keep on staying there.

In August of the same year, my grandma passed away too, and with her the female head of the family was gone also.

The ultimate punch came in January 2021 when Andrew told me that he wanted to separate.

At that moment a new journey started. I hit the ground and I am blessed enough to have friends and a family that helped me stand up, I am blessed to have this strong will, this temper, to be a warrior, to be tough, and I am specially blessed to have the opportunity to appreciate all those things.

I can say now that all those events happened for a reason, I wanted many things to go differently in my life, but some-time after that January 10th, I know that I am already living my best life. Of course, I would love to have my mother here with me, I guess it is not even necessary for me to say that. But what is important for me is that for the first time in my life I feel completely free. I feel that I did what I had to, and now I am doing what I want to, and I can't undo what is done, I will be forever divorced, I screwed my mandates in a way that can't be fixed, and it's so liberating!. As I said, I worked so hard to become an entrepreneur and a business woman, and now, I'm choosing to have the smallest team I've ever had, because at the same time I am the least stressed I've ever been, I am spending the most amount of time in self-care that I've ever done. I'm happier than ever. I am still that person, I still work hard, the difference is that I am learning how to live through honoring the responsibility of having options, and choosing what I really want to do for myself.

Someone told me one time "I am leaving this job because

I don't like it," and at that moment I thought, "Wow, she is so lucky she can afford to do what she loves."

At that moment I didn't even know what it was that I would love doing, I just remember having that thought, as well as disliking it. I didn't want to feel envy or any similar feeling, but I felt that way, and that discomfort stuck with me.

It's fine not knowing what would make us happy, as long as we don't victimize ourselves. This is important, we are not victims of our life paths or events, and through this understanding, we can own those moments, learn, and capitalize them. We can create our own desired life. I took that discomfort and found a way to create my desired reality.

Now I know better, she is not lucky, she is brave, she has commitment to her wellbeing, she has boundaries, and she made conscious choices.

Today I understand that each one writes its own path, many times consciously and many unconsciously, but that in the end, no matter how much we want to control a lot of factors, life takes us to where our deepest desires are, and the call of destiny. This book is about living your life consciously and proactively.

Consistently, throughout my life, I dedicated myself to doing things, to exploring, to learning, I was carried away by curiosity and I was discovering and developing different passions and abilities. Deep down, I am preparing to become my ultimate self.

Consistently in my life I made decisions that had a strong impact on my future. For example when emigrating. There were times when I thought "what am I doing here?" But I always focused on what I had to win and trusted that I was going to get ahead. Sometimes, I didn't know how things were going to be resolved, I felt frustration, anguish, anger with me, and despair, but I always got up and moved on, with the conviction that something better was going to come and with the certainty of the reason that led me to make the decision in the first place. I always had and still feel inside me (in my gut) that there is something more to discover, and since I have been coaching I feel that I have reached my destination. That this is the profession that fulfills me, and that it will continue to open doors for me in the future.

Something I learned from one of my soul sisters, Roman's mother (that's her name now) is: keep pushing forward, and at some point, the results all come together! Take a mother's advice, go on! Trust them, they know better! Why am I sharing this with you? Because at many points in my life I couldn't see the light at the end of the tunnel. There were moments when I didn't know how I would get where I wanted to be, or when the results of my hard work would pay off, as she said, keep on moving forward, it will all come together when the time is right!

Consistently, whenever I envisioned myself at thirty-three years old, I never envisioned her as fulfilled and happy as I feel now. I grew up believing that fulfillment came from the hand of getting married and having children; however, here I am, without my mother, separated from my husband, without children, and rediscovering myself with a version of me that feels enthusiastic and motivated again, a version that feels ecstatic with myself!

If you are reading me, believe me, we all have this version, and many times that version comes out in coaching sessions!

Because whenever your "now" is, it is the perfect time for you to receive this message.

I used to have a rule about books: I wouldn't start a new one until I finished the previous one. Until I noticed that it was preventing me from reading, sometimes I wanted to read, but not exactly that book. So I decided to break the rule and buy many books, different topics and some would be in Spanish and some in English.

I'm glad I broke that rule, because I learned that each part of each book has a different message, and those messages come to me in the perfect timing according to my mood. Also, I am reading way more than I used to, and it's a good way to connect with myself and check in about how I am feeling.

As I was planning the structure of this book, my wish for you was that you have the same experience I have when I read. So here's the plan: I have written in sections, and you can choose which section you feel like reading first. You should know that I organized it in a way that makes sense for me, but we all know that common sense is the least common of all, so I hope you connect with your own intuition and lead your own journey. I trust that your journey will be exactly as you need it!

In these pages, I share part of the experiences that led me here, what made me change my perspective and turn insecurities and weaknesses into confidence and strengths. How I came to be grateful for qualities like my temper and for the choices that I made that have been criticized in the past. How they gave me the strength and courage to keep on moving forward in the hardest times.

Each time I had an achievement I used to say, "If I could do it, you can also! I am not that special!" and each time there would be a confusion, I was not saying I wasn't capable, I was saying that I don't have any superpower. When I think about it, it is a kind of limiting expression, so I want to use this opportunity to rephrase it: "If I could, you can do it also! We are both that special!"

As you read, you will find out what "special" means. I will try to help you find and love each of those little parts of yourself that make you "that special." While thinking about "special," another word comes to mind, "extraordinary."

What is ordinary? According to the *Oxford English Dictionary*[1], it means usual, normal, or of no special quality. Then, extraordinary is everything that is above average, out of norm, special! All those extras that we all have in many different qualities, but sometimes we don't show them just because they are out of the standard. Please take a moment and think about all those extras that you have.

I recently uncovered I had an unconscious belief that I wasn't lovable just because I was too much. I talk too much, have too many opinions, and am pretty "bossy." I'm too naive, too independent, too strong, too sensitive, too loving, I laugh too loud, I am a lot! Now I know I am "extraordinary." See how it's already different?

It is awful that so many things had to happen to realize that all those characteristics make me be myself. I am just me. And all those things are the blessings I have that helped me overcome all those challenges and difficult moments.

In finding and getting to know ourselves, there's also the consideration of our image. It is part of the process to adopt a style that suits and represents us. The idea is to be different from others, to be just us. Over time, to be ourselves will be to forget about ourselves. We are born as unique individual beings. Over time we start to impoverish ourselves through the desire to belong to social stereotypes and groups.

When you think about yourself, what are the characteristics that make you who you are? What is your uniqueness about?

I found that the mix of all those things made me special, and each of us is special because we are all different. If we use those characteristics, we will build something accordingly. We all have the potential to create moments, things, love stories, lives, as unique as we are! So why would you stick to standards, expectations, or mandates if they don't even make sense, considering that there's no way that they make all of us happy? Social media is so focused on showing us models in different aspects that we almost forget that even those are characters. They are just people. Yes, they may have a couple of extra zeros in their bank account, but at the end of the day, they are just people.

Being just people means that they are not perfect; they go through life in the same way we do. They have their own feelings and stories. Being only humans means that there are only a couple of things in life that we can control. Still, we are all subject to all those things that we can't control, especially those things and events that money can't buy. So why would we keep thinking that there's an ideal way to be? Models just limit us and make us shrink to fit. Aren't you tired of making yourself small to fit? I am, and let me tell you, freedom is feeling so well already!

I am inviting you to a journey where you will find yourself and face the real you. I want to see you unleash your superpowers, double down in your talents, align with your heart and core beliefs, and create an impactful life!

I am inviting you to live on purpose! The time is now!

Before we start, I want to clarify that I wrote this book through my own filters. I speak from my own experiences and truths, and I always make sure that you know the source of information. This means that none of these are the only truth, perspective, or opinion, and I am eager to hear from you about your views, thoughts, and attitudes.

Please be aware that my intention is to make you uncomfortable, challenge your beliefs, and make sure that you know we are in a safe space. I opened my heart to you, and I challenged myself to be vulnerable in each chapter.

Be ready to feel the words in your chest and in your gut, and when that happens, it means that there's some work to do, so when you get there, take your time, and promise yourself to come back and start making adjustments, but don't look away. Choose discomfort. The comfort zone never brought anyone to the next level. Reach out for help if needed, but commit to your happiness and wellbeing because you are the only person that can make that decision. You are the only person that can make that happen.

Get ready to turn on that internal fire to create your own method, your strategies, and your plan, to shine brighter than ever.

Bring a pen or a pencil, and make sure you write your thoughts down to review them later.

Safe travels!

JOURNAL IT

II

GIFTS

4

WHAT IS A GIFT?

THIS BOOK IS ABOUT PURPOSE. I've spent a lot of time thinking of ways to describe purpose for people who have come to work with me. I thought I knew what it was, after everything I've been through to find mine. It turns out that writing about it in a way that others can relate and take action is a little different from living it or even from partnering with clients through the transformation one on one. It wasn't until I was asked to deliver a talk about purpose that I came to a simple formula:

PURPOSE = GIFTS + VALUES + PASSIONS + GOALS

Magic happens in the alignment! If you can bring all four pillars together, you can find and live *your purpose*. In this chapter, I'm going to explore what gifts are so you can start building up your first pillar.

Gifts:
• a thing given willingly to someone without payment; a present
• a natural ability or talent

The first thing you should know is that gifts are those talents given to you as a present. They are your superpowers. Some quick examples are:

- Playing beautiful music
- Being positive and seeing always the good
- Bringing joy
- Helping friends to solve problems

Your gifts are what make you "that special," and you should be proud of them. Many people go through life not knowing what their gifts are—some people don't even know that they have a gift! This was me when I was younger.

I grew up not believing in myself, feeling different from the rest of the people around me. So when I started to search for my gifts, it took me some time to acknowledge that some of those characteristics that have been criticized were actually my superpowers. For example, I've been called stubborn. In reality, my gift is my willingness to keep on moving forward. I am committed to myself to feel well and be happy, so no matter what, I will get up every morning and thrive. See the difference?

As we all learned, when we receive a gift, we are supposed to say, "thank you." It's a show of appreciation. When we think about our uniqueness as a gift, we can introduce "gratitude" as a regular practice.

You can practice gratitude in the best way that suits you. Some people do it in the morning, in their yoga practice, during the day. I prefer to do it at night, before going to sleep, and every time I face a challenge.

A couple of days ago I was having a pretty rough morning. On the way to my sister's home, I was driving through the highway and there was something on the floor that made the wheel break. So I took the car to the side and while I was thinking, "What is this about? What do I have to learn from this?" I called my sister to let her know that I was on the way but delayed, and she immediately told me "Gi, this is happening right now so you confirm how capable, strong and brave you are." It's funny how by saying that she gave me an answer for a question I didn't even ask her, but it changed the perspective of the situation, so I got empowered and grateful, mostly because I had a spare wheel and I managed to change it. So I did it, and went to her home safe and sound. Honestly, it was not as straightforward as I am writing it, but it was not a big deal.

When practicing gratitude we can turn every event into a blessing. Here, I'll share two moments that were game-changers for me:

1.

The first one was while talking with a team member. She was having a situation at home where her husband would get drunk and take her daughter (that was not his daughter) to go around in the car with his friends. I couldn't believe what I was hearing, because I would never let any drunk man take any girl with him and his friends. She was explaining to me that she was being unable to leave him, or to stop him, for whatever reason. There was no real reason, since other team members knew about this and we were all offering help, so it was just about her.

That day was the first day I was grateful for my temper. Her decision was not about resources, it was about her not being able to deal with the problem. Of course none of it made me feel well. However, it helped me appreciate the fact that I love and respect myself enough that I wouldn't let anyone treat me or my kids in that way (I don't have kids but I don't even want to get started on how protective I am).

Again, we can make a point on how we grew up and how we learn to live our lives in different ways, but the point here is that being in a gratitude state helped me realize that one of my "worst" qualities ended up being worth being grateful for. It became a strength.

2.

The second was when my mom passed away in February 2020. One of my friends told me "Only with time you will understand why this is happening now, trust me, God has a plan and there's a reason why things are the way they are." I was devastated and at the moment I thought it was silly, "how on earth am I going to be grateful for this?"

On March 16th, they closed the airports in Argentina. There was a pandemic. At those early stages I still couldn't think about being thankful for my mother's fate.

A year and a half later, (it was yesterday), we were having dinner with two of my siblings and at some point one of them said, "I can't imagine how painful it would have been for mom to go through this pandemic, I'm not even sure if she would have made it."

Many times through the pandemic I felt thankful for having the opportunity to see her, to share her last days together, to be able to be with her all the way and then come back home.

With these two events, I'm trying to share with you the importance of being grateful, all the time, no matter what, even when we don't know what to be grateful for, just know, God, fate, the universe, whoever you believe in, has your back and things happen for a reason. This doesn't mean that those things won't hurt us, but having faith and being thankful would help us to navigate those moments in the best way possible.

There are always highs and lows in life. When plans are not going as we wanted, it's because God or the universe have a better plan for us, so we need to surrender and trust that something better is coming. When we are in a low, is when miracles happen, again, God or the Universe will do their thing and help us move forward. We will always have the tools and resources to move forward on every stage of our life.

Going back to the gifts, I can't avoid thinking that a gift is a present, and The present, is *the present*: here and now. So for us to make the most of it, to make our presence count, it's important to have our head where we have our feet, to have our mind, body and heart connected and be fully present.

Present and Presence

Present:
• To make a gift to
• Now

Presence:
• the fact or condition of being present

I heard this many times from my coachees, and it happened to me also, so I feel it's important to share. When I said that we need to have our head where we have our feet what I meant was to avoid being thinking about something else that is not what's happening at that moment, it may be cooking, having a conversation, dancing, working, whatever it is that you are doing, it's a must to practice being fully present.

We spend a lot of time worrying about things that didn't even happen or that may never happen at all, so why would we use our time and energy on those thoughts, especially because they prevent us from enjoying the present.

Our presence also affects our performance in our professional life. To communicate better is indispensable to focus on the conversation. When doing presentations, I used to have a coachee that she would get so nervous that she wouldn't even know what she was saying, she would get stuck, she was having bad times. Until we started working together, she developed her public speaking skill and that helped her, not only to enjoy those presentations, but also to be fully present and able to answer any questions that people may have.

Worrying about the future also brings a lot of anxiety, I've seen and experienced it myself, so my suggestion here is to make plans for a small amount of time. I have this other coachee, he has a full-time job, a dynamic social life, and he is also studying. So at the end of the semester, while he was planning his finals, he showed up stressed thinking about how he would accomplish to finish the whole year and earn his degree in 2022.

We worked together on a plan for the whole month, June, and he stuck to it without thinking about anything further than that.

He completed that month as he was supposed to, sat for all the exams he planned to, and now he is thriving in the last semester of the year, working on a new plan that would take him to December.

According to Leahy, Study of Cornell University, scientists found that, firstly 85 percent of what we worry about never happens. Secondly, with the 15 percent of the worries that did happen, 79 percent of the subjects discovered that either they could handle the difficulty better than expected, or that the difficulty taught them a lesson worth learning.

The conclusion is that 97 percent of our worries are

baseless and result from an unfounded pessimistic perception.

For this reason, it is important to acknowledge that we can control our thoughts, we can choose what to think and prevent all those worries and anxiety. It is about training our brain to go through positive and solution-oriented paths.

Blessings

As I mentioned at the beginning of the chapter, we can turn every moment into a blessing through gratitude. So let's talk about this.

Blessing:
• God's favor and protection

Whoever your God is, make sure you acknowledge them and be grateful.

While talking with a friend of mine, I was telling her about how I feel that I am broken (not in an economic way), that my heart is broken and that I am being born again. That after these past years I am not the same person. And she told me that we are all broken at some point, because that is life, and that we need to be broken for us to be complete. A seed has to break before it grows. It's part of the process, and those hard and sad events of our life are our blessings, because they make us grow and evolve.

When we break, there are cracks on the surface of our autopilot daily routine. Then, light comes into our soul through those cracks, and once that light is hitting those new places, we can't undo it. Our priorities will change, our worries will change also, we are so used to living on autopilot that we don't take the time to go deep inside, so those moments that break our surface are blessings that would let us heal.

Healing comes from being broken, and from going deep inside our soul. It is hard, it is challenging, it is time and energy consuming, and requires commitment. Nobody can do the work for us; we need to make the decision and go through it. Grieving will be waiting for you, so avoiding it won't make any difference, you will be just postponing it. There are no rules to go through, but I am confident that with the right help we are fully capable of learning how to live our new life. And as a consequence, we will learn not only how to love in a different and evolved way, but also how to connect in a deeper way with our spirituality.

We normally associate gratitude, blessings, and gifts to straight positivity, at least I used to. Now, I associate them with opportunity, perspective, and a way of living my life. My intention is for you to appreciate not only the great things that we have and most of the times we take for granted, we even take ourselves for granted, but also to get to an appreciation point where you are truly going through your life understanding purpose. Understanding that everything happens for a reason and it is our challenge to see the good in those things, as I said, it may be hard and it may take time, but for me, life will never put you through something harder than what you can deal with. Furthermore, life will always give you tools and resources to navigate it. Again, it is our job to stay calm and open to make the most of each situation.

When looking for our gifts, my suggestion is to ask your best friends. The reason is that they love you just as you are. This means that they know and appreciate our superpowers, as well as our flaws. So, if you're struggling to find them, now you know where to start. As I think about it, in my experience it was super rewarding to ask them, so even if you know which are your gifts, take a moment and ask your best friends which they think your gifts are. I know you will be surprised.

Last but not least, I strongly encourage you to practice gratitude, it doesn't matter which way you prefer to do it, but start to practice it, chose an aspect of your life, let's say that you're not happy with your body, or with your job position, start being thankful every day for three things on those areas, and then, when you've been over each part, you can start to move to another area of your life, until you create a habit and it becomes an abundance mindset.

Here are some questions to reflect:

- What are your unique gifts, talents, or superpowers?
- If you are having a hard time finding them: Who have you been when you've been at your best?
- How often do you use your gifts?
- How would you like to use them more?
- How are you using those gifts in each area of your life?
- How are you creating an impact through them?
- How would you like to create an impact in a different way or area that you are not today?

JOURNAL IT

5

WRAP UP YOUR GIFTS

As WE SAW in the last chapter, gifts include many concepts, superpowers, and talents, present, presence. For us to unleash our superpowers and create an impact, we need to acknowledge them, to know how to expand them to different areas of our lives and to be capable of being fully present. The way I found to make the most out of each situation is to have my body, mind and heart connected. Through this connection I can always show up being my best self.

The importance of knowing our gifts is to be able to use them in the best way. As I said in the previous chapter, a gift is a present, and as it was given to us, I feel that it was given to us for a reason, and that's so we share it with others. It is our responsibility to use our superpower in the best possible way and create an impact in all the levels of our life.

So, through knowing ourselves, we get to accept and love each part of us. This is the key to the interactions.

Now that we understand the importance of wrapping up our gifts, we will dedicate this chapter to work on connecting these different aspects of our person.

I recently discovered that I've spent my whole life relating to most people from my insecurities, meaning that I was not showing up as myself. Instead, I was being the person that I thought I should be to belong to that place, and live up to certain standards. I am not talking about adapting, I am talking about pretending. I used to pretend that I liked certain things—events, places, people, attitudes, just to belong. I used to lie about my job position and my career, just because some guys felt intimidated by my professional life and my aspirations. All of this made me feel that I could not be myself, I wasn't being seen, heard, or loved for who I was. (Don't get me wrong. I'm not saying that there aren't men going through the same thing. What I am saying is that, in this period of my life, I wasn't being transparent and genuine in my interactions with people, particularly with men and it hurt me.)

Part of the problem was the lack of self-esteem, neglecting who and how I was, undervaluing what I have to offer, and letting other opinions affect me. We all should know that we don't need validation. If you don't know it yet, then, this is the sign you were looking for.

Now you know, you don't need validation!

Not long ago I realized that I had been trying to be seen and to get recognition from that part of the family that were loving me from their expectations, like my grandparents. As well as my older brother and sister. We were born within three years and a half, and it's crazy how our life experiences are so different, as well as our personalities. We've always been united and loved each other. However, we got to know each other through our own perspectives. This means that I used to feel that I wasn't a 100 percent myself around them, I used to feel that I wasn't enough for them, and my insecurities were constantly triggered, so they wouldn't get to know my real self, they would get to know the person I thought I should be to be around them. We are blessed to have had the opportunity to talk about all these differences in our life experiences, emotions, and perspectives, to relate and empathize with each other so our relationship got real, and our love stronger than ever. I'm happy to say that we are very close and united from a very genuine and respectful place now.

As for my younger sister and brother, I've always felt extremely seen and loved by them. I've always felt accepted just for being myself, I've always been real and genuine around them.

Each of my siblings taught me so many things about how to live my life. They've been great teachers and examples of bravely, humbleness, freedom, resilience, and evolution. I am so blessed to have them in my life, I know I wouldn't be here, and feeling this way if it wasn't for them. I know that no matter what, they will always be there for me, and that when I fall, they will always pick me up to laugh and to cry together, and they know I would do that for them also.

I need to respect, accept, and love myself first, then others will do it also.

My first step to love myself was to think and be specific about what I like and what I don't. I started to explore different activities, and to check how I was feeling about that. I was giving myself simple things that were making my heart and soul feel better.

Last December I went to New Orleans by myself. Andrew didn't want to come with me, but I knew it would be good for me, so I went anyway. It was beyond what I expected. What I found is that I am my best company and being with myself is enough. It was so easy to be with myself, I spent five days doing only what I wanted, and when I wanted it. I took some time to laugh, to cry, to enjoy music, to read, I did tours, walked, I ate amazing food, tried as many shoes and hats as I wanted, and most importantly, I felt well. I reconnected with myself.

So, the first step is to reconnect with yourself. Find little things that don't cost you anything and do them for yourself. I recommend spending time with yourself, however, I know that it's hard for some people, so baby steps are the key.

The first distinction here is that to be alone is different from being lonely. Actually, I'd rather say that I am with myself, it gives me and other people the clear feeling that I am not lonely, I am not sad, miserable or anything, I am choosing to spend time with myself, to enjoy my company. Have you ever felt lonely or sad when you were with people? This is a real thing, and I want to address it. Some people may think or feel that being with someone else is better than being alone, no matter how good or bad that other person is. When I went to New Orleans I was still married, and I didn't miss Andrew, that was the first moment when I thought that there may be something wrong, because I was having a blast with myself, and somehow, I knew that I wouldn't be having such a nice time if he was there. However, sometime after that, when I separated, I started to miss him. Here's the reflection:

What do we miss when we miss someone?

I thought I was missing Andrew. But what I was missing was having a partner, being loved, and accepted, having a healthy relationship. I wasn't having that in my marriage the last couple of months, then, what was I missing?

Identifying that I wasn't missing him, I was missing the relationship that we used to have, was a key to make progress and put everything where it belongs. I have room for a partner in my life, that is not emptiness, again, it is room, and the partner is not him anymore. Both of us are good people, it's just that we don't work well together as a couple.

So don't call the toxic, or any kind of ex that you have!

At least don't do it until you find out if you're missing the person or the relationship. Instead, you can visualize yourself in a new and healthy relationship and invest your time on yourself.

When missing my mother is different, I miss her. What comforts me is the fact that I know she is still here caring and protecting us, so there's no room for another mother, she is the only mother I will ever have in my life, so it's no room or emptiness, it's a transformation. Again, who I miss is her and all about our relationship.

As I said before, this may be a good exercise to organize your feelings. I also know that we can't help what or how we feel, but it's important to put the right labels on each feeling. And this is another step: to identify, label and embrace our feelings. Once we start being connected with ourselves, it may take some time to identify each feeling, at the beginning we will feel discomfort, in our chest or body, and then, we will start to recognize the feeling. Once we get there, we can start working on the route or trigger of the feeling.

For now, we will stick to connecting with ourselves and identifying our feelings.

This is also an example of how society triggers our insecurities, let's say that if you are alone, it is assumed that you don't have friends, family, you're lonely, bored, and sad. This is not true; this is just wrong judgement of a particular situation.

I recently came to the conclusion that insecurities come from judgement.

This is another step that helped me to love myself: Avoid judging and pre-judging.

There's a trick I found, since we judge from our insecurities, according to the standards and stereotypes we have in our head, the harder we judge others, the harder we will judge ourselves. This means that we use a different yardstick to evaluate ourselves. Therefore, if you start seeing others with love, you will see yourself the same way also. For this reason, I strongly encourage you to start with this practice ASAP. It was a game changer for me!

So, continuing with the example, next time you see someone by themselves, just assume that the person is enjoying her company, that the person is respecting and loving herself through doing what she feels like doing, and that she chose to be there by herself, it's not that she didn't have any option.

And then, for me, the more I discover myself and the closer I get to just being as I am, the more I accept myself, the more I enjoy myself, the more I discover that I am loved and accepted just as I am.

The fight was between the Gisela I am and the Gisela I believeed should be according to stereotypes and social mandates.

I normally call that other part of me that has all those extras "Ivana" (my middle name). "Gisela" is the person that shows up according to mandates and social expectations. During this journey, I am becoming more "Gisela Ivana" than one or the other. I am recognizing her and letting that unique part of myself be.

When I separated I felt that it was enough. At the end of the day I did everything I could to keep my relationship alive, but what I was not noticing is that in that journey I lost myself. I was so focused on the fact that it was so important to have a partner, even to have kids. I am conscious that I put my relationship through unnecessary stress because I kept on hearing about the age and the kids and all those things. If I'm being honest, there was some anxiety triggered by my mother's passing away so young, but that's another issue that I thankfully could acknowledge and figure out with my therapist.

During my relationship, many other things happened, including the fact that I lost myself, and in the search for my real self I changed. He told me that I've changed, and I couldn't understand how. I had connected with my most real and honest version, Ivana, I was not the same person. I had to lose myself to actually find myself. And through being unloved by someone else, I finally started to love myself properly.

It's taking me time, there were therapy sessions where I would say "I Don't even know what I like, or what I want right now, I am so sad and overwhelmed." It's not that I didn't know, it's just that I was so overwhelmed by the whole situation that I didn't know where to start. And that's ok!

Justo always encouraged me to take it step by step. I made a list with possible little activities that would comfort me, such as watching a movie, eating well, taking a bath, having my nails done, reading, walking, painting, simple things. I spent so much time doing huge puzzles, coloring books, my sister Barbara used to come every Friday to my house to do yoga practice, and we would do as much as I could, even if it was just stretching. Again, simple things that don't cost you anything. Always keep in mind that there are things that we can do to feel better, and there are things that we can do that will make us feel bad or worse. Loving yourself enough is to choose activities that will make you feel better.

Slowly I started to reconnect with myself. Other practices that helped me were to divide the day in small periods of time, so I would only organize the morning, the afternoon, or the evening. That practice combined with a frequent check-in such as "How am I feeling right now?" "What do I feel like doing?" helped me to reconnect my mind, body, and heart. I would listen to myself and follow my needs.

I reconnected with books, with my ukulele, with friends,

with dancing lessons, all that happened through exploration. I would go out by myself to eat, or to the beach, it didn't matter, it was all about reconnecting and getting to know myself better.

I'd like to encourage you to take a moment and make a simple list of those things that won't cost you anything and you can do for yourself.

When it comes to my professional life, I don't have the same insecurities. I built my confidence through my experience. When I was studying I used to start the final season sitting for Theology, because it was easy and through passing it I would feel empowered to keep on moving forward.

Nowadays, I still do the same, I challenge myself all the time to keep on learning and improving, and I do it through creating accomplishment experiences, I start with baby steps, building my confidence, and then, I move to the bigger challenges. I always take one challenge at a time, and make sure that I feel in my body and heart ready for it. It has to do with my energy, can I afford to face and overcome this now?. Expecting to be ready with your mind most likely will take you forever, at least I would never be ready in my mind, there's only a limited amount of knowledge and skills that we can accumulate, so we need to deal with that fact, and with the fact that we are not perfect and there's always room to improve.

You are already ready!

Through my professional life I left my comfort zone many times. The first one was when I started as a General Manager of one of the businesses of my family, I was twenty-three. Then, when I moved to the US and started a business from scratch with my sister, I was twenty-seven. The last time was when I started with my coaching practice, two years ago.

Each time there were many skills that I had to develop,

many new activities and tasks. When we came to the US, on top of being in a different country, it was a different system and a different language, that was so hard! I definitely underestimated the project, but if I had been realistic about it, I probably wouldn't have done it.

What helped me navigate those times was the knowledge on how to build my confidence. As I said, through experience, and when you don't have little or easy tasks to start with, or you are overwhelmed and you feel that everything that is going on is a lot, my advice would be to take a moment and make an accomplishment list. It's simple, you write down all the things that required effort, that you considered a challenge, and as a consequence, an accomplishment. Be honest with yourself, don't be hard on yourself, just be honest and write those tasks and activities down!

Going back to the example of spending time with yourself. Let's say that you want to go out by yourself, so you get dressed, you get in the car, and when you arrive at the place, you park but you don't leave the car, you don't get inside the place, that's fine, it is progress, it is accomplishment! So, appreciate those steps!

There's a salvation to make, please consider only the things that you wanted to accomplish, don't take into account anything else, don't think about anything that you didn't accomplish because you didn't want to, or anything that may seem like a failure (we will come back with this later).

Keep that list close to you, and I promise you, every time that you doubt yourself, as soon as you go through your accomplishment list you will feel empowered and confident.

How do I feel when I am connected?

How do You feel when you are connected?

While I was grieving it was hard for me to understand what was happening to me. I found an email I sent my doctor two months after my mom passed and it said "I am not doing well; I am not feeling well. Nothing is hurting me, and everything is hurting me, I am extremely sad. Every week I am feeling worse, I miss her so much." I remember that I couldn't focus, my brain wouldn't work. I was feeling that my body and my brain were working at 30percent of their capacity.

Sometime after that, I would start to push myself to get better, again. I wasn't understanding that I had to just be and that time will make things better. In my life, every process I've been through, I would understand it, find a way or a solution, and move forward. I've always rationalized the challenges and difficulties. But this was different, there was nothing to figure out, there was no solution. It was the first time I faced something so permanent. Nothing is permanent except for life and death. With this confusion I would push myself, and then feel worse, because tiredness was an add on to the feeling.

Eventually, I accepted that this was the new reality, that I didn't know how long it would last, but I needed to be patient and compassionate with myself, so I committed to do my best while respecting my energy and mood. Each day I would choose only a couple of activities that would be simple and impactful, some days it would be just getting out of the bed, taking a shower, getting dressed and completing the tasks I had for work.

One day, Andrew found me working late, and consequently being tired and sad, so he asked me "When was the last time you checked in with yourself?" I wasn't even sure if I had ever checked in with myself. Then, I started to ask myself many times a day "How am I feeling?" "What do I feel like doing now?" and I would give myself whatever I wanted. This includes working with a doctor to check and organize my diet, and in this process, fasting is something that helped me a lot, because I started to acknowledge when I was feeling hungry, and then eating through intuition, it's simple, but a real connection. I did it with a doctor so don't take this as advice, please check with a specialist before doing any change in your eating habits. As I was connecting more and more with myself, I started to identify what circumstances were comfortable for me, and which were not. I wasn't feeling like meeting with a lot of people, going to some places, eating certain foods. And it became a habit. I even started thinking ahead, this year for my birthday I was recently separated, so again, I wasn't feeling like a big celebration, and I knew my sister would encourage me to do something bigger than what I wanted. Therefore, I decided that I wanted to go out with her, her husband, and a friend of mine to have dinner that day, and so we did. I had such a great time, and I was especially happy because I gave myself the time to connect my mind, my body, and my heart, and respected them!

Now, as I am working from home, I work around my schedule to make sure that I am fully connected and showing up ready and in the best way possible for each session. For that purpose, I need connection. I have a coachee on Sunday's night, it is the best time for him, and as we had been working together for a long time, I do the exception, the problem for me was that I was finding it difficult to match his energy, and I told him that, so he had the choice of keeping the slot or changing to another day. He wanted to keep the slot. After giving it some thought, I tried going for a run before the session, a short run, and that helped me to have my energy up, and it became a routine. What is even better, is that going for a run on Sundays put me in a better mood for the week, so it ended up being good for me also!

Being fully connected with yourself will help you to identify your moods, your feelings, what each activity is providing for you, how each moment is impacting in your presence. And through identifying those things, you will be able mindful and bring the energy purposely.

I invite you to take a moment and think about how you feel on different circumstances or moments through your day. This requires a lot of awareness, so if it's hard for you to recognize those feelings, then you can start by taking a couple of minutes some time during the day and reflect on your yourself, on your mood, your energy, and your mind. Check the kind of thoughts you are having, and how those thoughts make you feel, and then, you will be able to choose those exercises that bring the best out of your mind, body, and heart.

In my experience, it was a path, it took me time, I had to be intentional at the beginning, and now it has become a habit. It has an impact on my eating habits, organization, energy, and social life, because as part of respecting myself, I stay where I am until I feel like leaving. If I feel tired, or that is late and the program will have an impact on the following day, I would leave. I choose how long I will run, or if I'd rather go to the gym. Checking-in and respecting myself became my absolute priority, including having some "me" time, which I appreciate a lot!

Many of my coachees are going through the connection process. Learning to communicate what we want is also a key to the process. So the plans can be adjusted as all the people participating want. I am talking about Mr. E. His homework was to take some time and ask himself what he wanted to do, and then communicate properly with his girlfriend, so they could make a plan accommodating both wants and needs.

I'll give you some context, they had a plan, and there was a last-minute change. He wanted to do both things, but instead of communicating that, or the fact that he was waiting for that Sunday to come and go to see the movie that was being released that day, he just went to the last-minute plan with a long face. He could have had fun with that plan, and then gone to the cinema. However, he chose to show up bothered and missed the movie.

When he came back the following session, he had tried it many times, and he had the opportunity of acknowledging how he was feeling. Through communicating, he was able to adjust the plans or circumstances, and show up being in his best mood. Then, his answer to "What did you discover during this process?" was "That being myself and doing what I want is healing and freeing." This doesn't mean that he was not adjusting, this means that he stopped denying his feelings, and started to share them with his partner.

I couldn't have expressed it better or agreed more!

How do you feel when you are disconnected?

Another coachee answered this one. Meet Peter. He is a successful entrepreneur, who built his brand from scratch, and part of the fuel to doing so was the fact that he was bullied as a teenager.

Every time Peter was meeting his friends from high school he would end up having anxiety and feeling uncomfortable. He couldn't explain what it was, so we started the exploration.

He came to the conclusion that he was disconnected from himself, and not setting boundaries properly. He was talking more than he wanted, he was finding himself saying things that would come out in a way that he didn't mean, he was having doubts and old insecurities, but he wasn't finding the triggers yet.

Peter is still in the process, but what we know so far is that part of the triggers came from the old belief of him not being enough, of being bullied over being nice and gentle, so when people asked something, he had the need to show off, even though showing off was not his style, or how he normally is.

My disconnection felt different.

When there's a painful situation, I disconnect myself to avoid suffering. It's not that I miss the signals, I just ignore them and keep on moving forward until the situation explodes in front of me.

For instance, when it comes to my mother's health, I knew what was going on, but I was hyper focused on her recovery, I couldn't acknowledge the real situation, it was too painful, so I protected myself. Then, when I couldn't avoid facing it anymore, the pain was still there, waiting for me, and I started wondering how I missed all those red flags, until I realized that I haven't missed them, my heart and body always knew what was happening, it's just that my mind was not acknowledging the feeling, while my body was. My mind was keeping me moving forward, until it couldn't anymore.

In conclusion, I have a disconnection between my body and it's sensations and the real problem. I know that there is a problem but for some reason I don't face it, or acknowledge it. I let it build up until I can't take it anymore or it explodes. It's a survival mechanism.

How do we connect?

Through paying attention to our own experience. First, we need to start being more aware of the triggers. Intentionally get uncomfortable with things that we don't like, or may hurt us.

Then, we need to strategize around those triggers, and make sure we have a plan for those moments that make us feel uncomfortable, so through awareness and readiness Peter started to manage those moments well.

Those changes required him to be fully aware of his feelings and be ready to be brave if needed. After a couple of meetings with his friends, he was making solid changes. We would talk and find those triggers, think about how he would answer in his own way while feeling comfortable. His awareness was rising, so he was better at instantly recognizing and addressing those triggers, and after each meeting he was feeling better, and more like himself, without that anxiety.

As a consequence, he enjoys going to the meetings now, and he is relating with them from a different position than he used to.

When it comes to me, I learned that if my body is not feeling comfortable, then I need to observe and go over the information I received to check what may have hurt me or what I may not like to hear. Then, I would have to face it! Sometimes those things that give me anxiety are not necessarily something bad, it can be something that was said and I missed, or some energy. Once I find what it was I rationalize it, if possible, and talk about it with the person who triggered me, or with someone else that can help me get a different perspective on my perception. I'm talking about people I trust, and the purpose is to feel well, not to gossip. Then, I get back to being centered. If talking it through wasn't an option, then it was something insignificant I would let go.

Everything that I've been saying in this chapter has to do with self-love, because through loving ourselves we will be fulfilled. And it is in that energy level when we can shine bright and use all those gifts that were given to us. It is only through self-love that we can see ourselves just as we are, embrace and love every single part of our person and make our presence meaningful. Through connection, being centered and aligned with ourselves we will be fully present. And again, from there we will be ready to share with other people our gifts, to use them exponentially to create an impact.

How?

Loving ourselves enough to be our best version is from my point of view the number one priority.

There is a reason why we are required to put on our oxygen mask before helping others. And the reason is that we can help others if we are alive, if we are comfortable and being ourselves from love and respect.

Self-love is a priority, and the only way we can get there is through knowing ourselves. For that reason I think it is important to explore and define our gifts, to have good self-esteem, to be able to work and give our confidence a boost, to be connected mind, body, and heart. It is only this way that we will be able to show up being our best version, and living in the constant cycle of improvement. A gift is nothing if it's not shared.

This is how we wrap up our gift and make the most out of it!

As I was in a coaching session with Peter today, he was telling me that a girl he is dating triggers insecurities, anxiety, anguish, he wasn't even being himself around her, he's been miserable and unable to focus for the past ten days. Then I asked him if she was triggering those insecurities, or if he normally has them, he said he used to have them, but not anymore. I kept on making questions,

"What is good about this relationship if you so miserable?"

"She is extremely pretty; I think I like her"

"Do you like her for the person she is or as a trophy?"

"I probably like her as a trophy…"

And then, an AHA! Moment hit him. He realized that she was not triggering it, his feelings have absolutely everything to do with his old insecurities and beliefs of not trusting himself, not being enough, and consequently, the need to show to everyone that he was the best, and part of being the best was to date the prettiest girl, even if she was not bringing joy to his life.

In the end, we ended the session talking about what is important for him as a person. What are his values? How does he want to be the best? In which way? And with the homework of making a list of the qualities that he considers that make him be the person he is.

I could clearly empathize with this; I've been another side of this coin. I adapted to be with someone because I felt that he was adding happiness to my life, so as I said at the beginning of the chapter, I adapted and lost myself to make sure he loved me, and that's probably the main reason why he stopped loving me. I did it out of insecurities and holding the belief that I didn't deserve to be loved because of the way I am.

In this situation, Peter is with a person that is not adding happiness to his life, she is even making him miserable, but still, he is not being himself to make sure she loves or at least likes him. He is doing it out of insecurities and holding the belief that he was not enough and he had to prove otherwise.

What happens when you are the trophy?

There can be many ways to become a trophy, I will talk about the understanding I am having after observing and feeling this way in different moments. I am not talking specifically about romantic relationships; this applies to all the relationships.

When someone is seeing us according to the addition that we are to their lives in terms of presuming about us, they are not really seeing the person we are, they are seeing what we represent for them. We become objects that enlarge the other person's ego and self-esteem. The problem is that eventually, that person gets tired, because as we are seeing with Peter, they are not even being themselves, but they are having that relationship for a different reason.

After talking with people being in that situation, some of the common phrases are that the person doesn't pay attention to them, until someone else is interested. The person doesn't let them talk, doesn't listen, have some negative energy in the sense of not being supportive and creating more insecurities and doubts. These people have the feeling that the partner wants to be with them because of how they look like and the potential kids they may have. And of course, the person shows off them.

Being seen by someone has to do with being seen and appreciated for who you are just for yourself and not in relation to another person, it's not about who you are in terms of another person, not as a daughter, mother, father, wife, husband. People like me, that used to feel invisible and used to believe that wasn't enough, tend to relate to people that through paying all this attention make us feel special and seen, but eventually they get bored, because we become just an object, we were just a trophy. What is even worse, you were most likely adapting to be loved.

It is important to identify this because as we are talking about gifts, and how to use them in the best way, it is key to be surrounded by people that let us shine as bright as we can, when you are not seen, you become a shadow. So take a moment and ask yourself what you mean for other people, and how does it feel to be really seen?

The last recommendation of the chapter is to double check how you are relating to others, and then, which is the belief that you are holding that is making you act this way.

Let's go over the exercises:

First of all, in the last chapter we review how to explore your gifts through asking your best friends, make a list of accomplishments and explore activities that don't cost you anything and will make you happy.

In this chapter we are working on connecting with ourselves, mind, heart, and body.

We will start through identifying what we like and what we dislike, so after each of the activities that you have been exploring, take a couple of minutes and reflect on your mood and energy. After each meeting with friends, dates, or partners, reflect. I even suggest setting random alarms and check in with yourself, your mood, and feelings. Choose those actions that have a better impact on you, and discard those that have a negative impact.

Then, when we know what we want and like, it's important to communicate it properly, in a good way, we can start sharing with others and work on making plans that satisfy everyone. Keep on checking.

Last, but not least, identify triggers to those feelings that you dislike and explore the patterns on those triggers. Here are some questions to help you do that:

- How am I feeling? – label the feeling
- When do I feel like this?
- Who is triggering this feeling? How? – It's normally on us, not on other people, people are mirrors, they do or say something, the impact those actions have is on us.
- What does this trigger mean?
- What is the limiting thought or belief behind this feeling?
- How can I make it better next time?
- What do I need to do to feel better in this situation?

JOURNAL IT

III

PASSIONS

6

MEET YOUR PASSIONS

Passions are interests and skills that are best developed over time.

Passion:
• An intense desire or enthusiasm for something.

The idea that we have only one thing we are meant for, limits us from fulfilling our greatness. Each thing we do brings joys, but none of them are the purpose, they are passions.

Passions are created and developed, and we can have as much as we want. As I was saying, to build or create a passion, we need to start by choosing an activity that we like doing, or we think that we may like, and start to practice it consistently. The more we practice, the better we perform it, and the better we perform it, the more joy and fulfillment it will bring to us, and at that point is when it becomes a passion.

Thinking this through an example, we think we may like playing the guitar, so we buy the instrument. The passion will come when we learn how to play. The passion is not there the day we buy it.

To find our passion we may need some exploration on different activities, and even job positions that require different skill sets.

When we are developing a skill set that would let us perform passionately, we need to acknowledge that there will be a learning process also.

For us to create we need to have many ideas. I personally don't know a person that had only one good successful idea, maybe you know a person like that, however, most of us need to have many ideas to have one that is good, so be patient with the process and hold on to the fact that over time you will find that activity or skill that brings joy to you, and consequently to others.

Passions get even better when combined with gifts. Let's say that you are a good motivator, you may find a passion as a public speaker. It's just that to become a public speaker, you will need to develop a career, so, as I said, be patient, trust the process and always keep your heart open to new experiences.

If you don't know how to find your passion, you can start checking your gifts, and following your heart. If you are good at something, double down the time you spend doing that. Many passions don't pay for a lifestyle immediately, but eventually, you can build a business that would let you live from that passion.

My parents used to tell us "Go to university and study whatever you want, you will see later how you earn your money." And they were right, Fiorella is an Industrial Designer, and she manages her own company now. Barbara is an Architect, she has a master's in architecture also, and she became a yoga instructor in 2020. Now she is working to combine both passions into one project. Juan is studying engineering, he also developed an app, and is a trader. Maxi is an Industrial Engineer; he is managing his business where they design and build objects in iron.

As for me, I'm a passionate person. I love learning, working with people, motivating, helping others achieve their dreams, and also, I am into getting to know people's stories, and societies stories.

Through the combination of all those passions, I became a coach. I've been managing businesses for almost ten years, before starting my coaching practice. When I was studying business I never ever, not even in my wildest dreams, thought that I would be capable of writing a book. I identify a limiting thought, I used to say that "I am a numbers person," I am, and also, I'm finding out that I can write.

I am coming from a family that believes in formal education, so we had to go to university. My understanding is that this form of education is the tool some people found that was good to give their kids to move forward in their professional lives. Nowadays, things are slightly different. I am not under-valuing formal education; I am saying that it's not the only way to get results. "Informal" education, or self-education, is as powerful as the other. It all depends on how committed we are to learn and get results.

With this being said, the conclusions are that we never know in which way what we are doing today will help us in the future. Also, the importance of doing things consistently, so we go from amateur to master, until it becomes a passion. For this, we need to trust the process, and become friends with the patience and discomfort that learning and devel-oping a new skill requires and brings.

Another example that is coming to my mind, many years ago I took sewing classes. I wanted to do it because my mom took those classes before and so we could sew together. I know how to do it, but I don't practice it a lot.

Next month my sister is getting married, and to my surprise, I have the honor of creating her skirt (don't worry it's for the small celebration, not for the big wedding). What I mean is that even when we learn something that may seem useless, the fact that we developed that skill gives us the opportunity to do things that would bring great emotions. It may not be the activity I am most passionate about, but my passion grows because it lets me participate in those special moments in different ways, moments that we will forever cherish.

The line between exploring activities and having our schedule packed is pretty thin.

What I mean is that as we are, it is important to do. And for us to be able to do it in the best way, we need to be conscious. Check chapter 5 to know how to be fully connected and show up being your best version to each moment.

During a workshop about purpose, we were talking about passions. I gave the people in the workshop one follow up session. And there she showed up, Julie. She contacted me because after battling cancer, and being cancer free, she felt passionate about life more than ever. The problem was not having too many passions. The problem was that because of her willingness to be everywhere, and to participate in every event or social project she could, she overscheduled herself. Yes, she was living through her passions, but she was never fully present. She was frustrated with herself because she couldn't understand if it was possible to be that passionate and enjoy so many things, but she was also tired. She didn't notice that through being everywhere, she was nowhere.

So, by the end of the session she discovered that her actual passion was "living," and she committed herself to respect her energy, to schedule properly, one thing at a time, and to embrace all her passions and keep on enjoying them.

Passions are also dreams. As we are learning what we like, and we have more experience on specific activities, but also more experience about life, we get involved in different projects, and somehow we get in a path that takes us to accomplish those dreams. Even the dreams that we wouldn't dare to dream. Like me!

I've always been insecure, as you already know, and when I moved to the US I was especially insecure about my English. I'm fine with my accent, I was not fine with my fluency and vocabulary. Of course, I was always feeling short of vocabulary, it's different than speaking my first language. I worked hard to overcome this insecurity and frustration. Studying coaching was one of the activities I decided to practice since I needed to speak more, to incorporate more vocabulary and to be exposed to native speakers.

And look at me now, being a full-time coach and writing these lines. As I said before, I am closer to numbers, I never liked reading and writing parts, and yet I am here.

Passions are also related to habits, since habits are the best way to incorporate regular behaviors.

Habit:

- A settled or regular tendency or practice,
  especially one that is hard to give up.

As the definition from Oxford Dictionary indicates, habits are regular practices, that means that we have consistency and constancy, and also, they are hard to give up. Good habits are virtues and bad habits are vices. It's important to try to stay as much as possible on the virtues side, and this can be done by choosing what and how to develop.

At some point in my life, in my early 20s I found that reading was a habit I wanted to develop, because it helps to develop creativity, as well as nurturing other skills, so I started to work on my reading habit. As I mentioned at the beginning of the book, I used to read one book at a time, until I started reading many different books at the same time.

When I moved to the US, reading became more important since I had the need of incorporating more vocabulary and expressions, so I kept on working on that habit. All those books, and years of reading, lead me to a great amount of improvements.

First of all, I learned that the right book will come to me at the right time. Many books helped me overcome challenging situations.

Then, the more I read, the more I understand different topics and the better conversations I can have.

Also, I can learn to help my coachees with book recommendations and other lessons that those books would bring to me.

I never thought that all those books would lead me to where I am, and obviously, it was not just about the books, it's my whole journey, but I am sure that all the books I read are making a difference and had an impact on many levels of my person. All those great things I got from each book are motivating me now to write my own. And it's my deepest wish that it helps others in the same way many authors helped me.

Passions are not the exception when it comes to commitment.

Commitment:

- 1. the state or quality of being dedicated to a cause, activity, etc.
- 2. an engagement or obligation that restricts freedom of action

I picked these two definitions from Oxford Languages,

because together they illustrate what, for me, is the essence of commitment: Dedication and restriction of freedom or action.

When we have a commitment it means that eventually we will have to choose between that cause or activity and another. To keep the engagement and commitment with yourself to move towards your dreams and passions is what will make the difference. It has to do with "going the extra mile," a lot of people are talking about that, and I'm bringing it up now because it's definitely the difference. When you align your commitment with your goals, then you will get to the best result ever!

It was recently, in a coaching session with my editor that I came to a better understanding of these expressions: "going the extra mile" and "unleashing the power within." Those expressions are talking about the specific moment when you choose how to deal with the uncomfortable tasks, the laziness, and the activities that you don't like. How we get in charge, and deal with the discomfort is what will make the difference. It is the point where you did enough to reach the requirements and the standard, and then, it's about choosing to go all the way to be above average.

We need to commit to the process, to the uncertainty of what this development may bring in the future, where it will take us. The fact that we don't know how long it will take to master it. And the certainty that we are committing to our happiness.

A lot of times I hear people complaining about the difficulties and challenges they face on a daily basis, especially on working towards something they are trying to achieve. I hear them trying to get to their dreams with shortcuts, or to be experts without taking the time to learn and have the expertise. I hear excuses, putting the responsibility somewhere else or blaming others.

Let's get real on this, it requires being brave to have big dreams, and it also requires hard work, consistency, commitment, and constancy. I know that we live in an era where things are so fast that we get frustrated by waiting for a couple of minutes. Way more than what we need is a click far from getting it tomorrow. Regardless of this, understanding that big dreams are the sum of small dreams, and that they require sacrifices and to put in hours of work, will help us to make a plan, stick to it, and celebrate the accomplishments that we are getting on the way.

Dare to dream, and dream big! And dare to do what it takes to get there, I know you can, and you know that also, but knowing that you are capable won't make it happen.

I've seen brilliant and talented people so many times lacking constancy and losing opportunities. Time goes by, and they are still in the same place, or make small progress compared to their potential.

I've never been one of those people, but I had the honor of coaching one of them. Meet Alexis, he is smart, handsome, he has great conversation, he is driven, and he grew up in a family that expected him to be nothing less than the best. They treated him as if he was the one and only.

In one of our last coaching sessions, he realized that his lack of constancy had to do with the fact that he's been treated in such a special way, that when things get hard, or when he doesn't want to do what he must, he would abandon. He became capricious, he didn't learn how to fight for what he wanted. He realized that many opportunities were given to him without him even asking for them, or without doing any merit. He never had to prove that he could, they not only expected him to do it, but also, they expected him to excel in his performance.

All this pressure, plus the easiness and fastness of his

accomplishments, made him move forward without having to battle.

For Alexis the development of this skill has a different root but finding how his life experience contributed to this was liberating for him, because now he can tackle those old beliefs and find new ones that would help him move forward in a better and solid way.

Have you ever heard any talented person being successful (meaning that they made a career based on that talent), saying that they got to those results easily and without having to give up anything? If you have, I would like to hear who that person is. I never had, that's why I think that it is more important to do the work than to be brilliant or to have talent.

We all have a superpower; we just don't invest in it enough to make it as special as it could be.

Talented people work at least as hard as all of us, the difference is that they convert their talent or superpower, into their passion, and that's an extremely powerful combination, think about the best football player or singer or whatever artist or activity they may be performing.

Life is a road, making consistent and intentional choices is what would make the difference. And yes, it is about working hard, but mostly, working smart!

If you are having a hard time finding your passions:

- What do you love/enjoy doing? Where do you spend your time?
- What makes you feel good?
- What are you good at? => Double down here!!!
- What do you like about your job?
- What does your job combined with your passion look like?
- How close are you to that vision?

- What could change to get you close to that vision?
- What are you willing to give up to make that vision your reality?

I'd like to challenge you to start something new. Choose something that you would never have chosen but you would love to try, as in the example with the guitar.

Take some time, discuss it with friends, partners, whoever you want, and start doing something new. Find a way of holding yourself accountable, and make it happen.

Consider this the beginning of a new passion.

I hope you share it with me!

JOURNAL IT

7

DARE TO CREATE

WE ENDED the last chapter starting a new activity that potentially could become a new passion.

What happens along the road, as we are moving through life? What happens is that we change and evolve, we grow, we learn. This is why in this chapter we will go over some of these concepts and find out how we adapt to those new stages in life through new beginnings, changes, and endings.

Many times in my life some of my closest friends and siblings pointed out the fact that I've changed in a positive way, the expression itself wasn't sounding well, it meant that I've evolved, and they definitely meant well, even though it was coming out weird.

At those moments I used to feel terrible about myself, specifically about the person I used to be, and that would give me some anxiety, and guilt.

Until this year, when someone told me "you are dealing with your break up well, it would have been terrible if this had happened two years ago," and, of course, I felt pretty bad, until I realized that it was actually good, and that the expression itself didn't even make sense.

I used to think that those comments had to do with lack of empathy, like "Why don't you try to observe how my life was and who I was at that point, instead of criticizing or giving an opinion?" and then, I realized that they wouldn't know how I was feeling or what I was going through in those periods of my life if I didn't share those feelings with them.

So I started sharing some sensations, feelings, difficulties, and other factors of the reality I was experiencing at those moments, and then, I found the empathy I thought they were lacking. My brothers and sisters empathize with me and expressed the surprise it was to find out that through my filters my reality was looking that different than theirs.

I strongly recommend expressing those feelings to heal. It is up to each of us, and the fact that it worked for me, doesn't mean that it will work for you, however, there's no loss in trying. I even considered to stop sharing my feelings at all, but that wouldn't have helped, that would have created more space and lack of understanding.

In the end, life is like going to the gym, you start curling your biceps with some weight, and then you move to a higher and higher weight. We are all capable of evolving, it's just that not all of us are looking forward to it.

As I normally do, I'd like to invite you take a moment and think about your evolution process:

- How willing are you to evolve, grow and change?
- Which skills have you improved?
- Which skills would you like to keep on developing?
- Which of those are potentially passions?
- How can you expand them and create an impact through them?

In a conversation with one of my sisters on the beach,

she shared with me this idea that we are all at different stages of our evolution, and that we are all going up in an elevator and each of us leaves the elevator in different floors. So what happens is that we may match our evolution with some people in some moment and then, a turn in events takes us or them to another floor.

The "forever" idea is nice, and the changes and endings tend to have a bad connotation, but trust me, it would be easier if we could understand that they are natural parts of cycles. Just think about it, as every day starts, it comes to an end, the same happens with seasons and years, it's the natural cycle.

Going back to evolution, I became passionate about learning the story of the cities and people. Every time I visit a place I find that people respond to patterns according to the culture, and that each culture has different evolutionary levels, as well as families. It's not the same to be the first, second or third generation in a place after immigration. It's not the same to have been born and bred in the same place, or to have a story of degrees or wealth in the family. Those details won't make us more or less people. However, those stories will shape our life experience, our beliefs, thoughts and then our behaviors.

From my perspective, we learn in a singular way, as a person, individually, and then, we also receive some knowledge from our family and from our social exposure, I mean culture.

To learn and evolve are skills. We can develop them, what we need is to have the intention and explore the ways we can make that happen. Life is not teaching each of us in the same way, there are different learning styles, so it makes sense that we all need and prefer different experiences and activities to learn.

To practice those skills you can start by observing others,

and making a list of the activities you would like to try, books to read, podcasts, videos, consume good quality content, explore from curiosity, even when we don't know what some information will add, in the end, those little pieces of knowledge get together into a new learning.

There are some people who don't believe in changing, they would say "I am 'this way', take it or leave it," and that phrase only reflects stubbornness. I've witnessed old people learning, changing their minds, adapting. My eighty-five-year-old grandma, my "Yiayia," set an amazing example through adjusting to the new reality. Yes, she expected us to be married and have kids in our 20s. But she's been extremely supportive when we decided to move to another country, she even visited us, and she stopped asking us for the expectations that she used to have. She grew up with a different mindset, and when she found out that some decisions she made had hurt some family members, she owned her actions, scheduled a meeting with us, her grandkids, her son, and daughter-in-law, and not only apologized, but also made amendments. So being too old it's just an excuse, there's no such thing as being too old to change or adjust. I am proud of her and honored to be her granddaughter.

When I was studying coaching, the instructors made a point about the importance of the coachee reaching out. At the beginning I didn't expect it to be a big deal, I couldn't see exactly why that was important, until I found out. Some people are close minded, they refuse to change their perspective, to learn or evolve. Coaching is a lot about that, and not everyone is ready for that process. And that's fine, I am not judging them, what I am trying to say is that as always, there are points of view, and once again, those who are willing to do the work, will make the difference in their lives also. Those who are not willing to do the work, then, they shouldn't complain either.

Nowadays, when someone tells me that I've changed I feel "flattered," I take it well, and I am grateful for being able to do it. Only people that take leaps of faith, that face challenges, that pay attention and intentionally learn, only they know how hard it is.

If you are one of those people, I see you! Don't feel guilt or shame about the past, feel grateful and happy for the person you became through all those experiences.

Let's move to some concepts that I feel will help in this evolution process.

Creativity:

- the use of the imagination or original ideas, especially in the production of an artistic work.

Constancy

- the quality of being faithful and dependable.
- the quality of being enduring and unchanging.

Consistency

- conformity in the application of something, typically that which is necessary for the sake of logic, accuracy, or fairness.

Of all the skills and habits, I chose these three because I strongly believe that are key for success.

Success can be any accomplishment in any form that may have for you. If you still don't know how success looks like for you, then you can start there:

- What does success look like for me?
- What does success mean for me?

So, I will go over the three of them, starting from creativity.

I used to believe that a person was born with or without it, but everything changed the day I learned that creativity is skill and can be developed. It was a game changer.

I chose to talk about it because many times in my coaching sessions I hear people saying just that "I am not a creative person," so I want to make sure that someone is telling this to you, and this is the only way I find to do it.

We all know that kids are more creative. It is my understanding that it has to do with the lack of structures and limits that we all learn as we are growing up. This doesn't mean that we will lose our creativity along the way, this means that we can find different ways to stimulate our brain and body to have new experiences and let the creative process begin.

Well, now you know that creativity is a skill!

As every skill we can all develop it, the question is HOW?

For me the answer is through the exploration of different activities, disciplines, experiences, and all the things that would help us in our particular learning processes.

It's fair to say that greater ideas come from teams. For me, the best ideas always come from passionate interactions where we all share different perspectives, and in that interaction, thoughts are provoked.

Also, creativity has to do with the mix of ideas that would cross your mind, so the most you have stimulated your brain and your body, let's say through travelling, through experiences such as roller coasters, skydiving, reading, watching movies, concerts, music, going out to different kind of places, museums, food, sports, talking to people, and all the universe of activities we can do, the better, because for the creation of a new concept, product, idea, experience, we need to recreate or be able to imagine what is it what we would like for the final outcome to be.

From my perspective, creativity in grownups has to do with putting together different ideas in a new way that was not done before, or even if you are taking an idea and you are adding your own touch to it, it's still creativity, the question is "how do we have that new idea?" or "where do we get those stimulus that would trigger the thinking process?"

Before answering those questions, there's a piece of clarification, it doesn't have to cost you anything, at least not necessarily. That's normally the first excuse, the second one has to do with time, and that one will be addressed later.

So, for you to explore those activities, I will mention the ones that come to my mind right away, reading, watching creative tv shows, food, drinks, languages, travelling, any adventure such as skydiving, meeting new people and hearing their stories, playing an instrument, visiting museums, or going to concerts. Also, as I said before, in my experience, the best ideas come from teamwork, and this supports this idea that creativity is to put together some ideas that were not put together in that way before. In the interaction of the team, and the mix of different life experiences, there are the best creative processes, just think about the synergy that is created when a team is working together, the amount of ideas is exponentially superior

I always keep in mind that every time we start to practice a new discipline or to learn something completely new, let's say that I start studying German, or to play piano, I've never done either of them, it would be beneficial for the brain, since it would be stimulated in a different way. So remember this: every time we start a new discipline, it's a great benefit for our brain.

Last, but not least, creativity will come out of being focused and connected to our creation. There may be a creation process, there are places, songs, drinks, food, dances, that would give us the creative mood, so don't wait for it just to come, set yourself up for success, get ready, try your process, and commit to bringing the best outcome you can, because at the end of the day, it is about showing up being your best version to deliver the best. Dare to be yourself, and vulnerable. As long as you do it with your heart, there will be an impact. And stay humble, if you touch just a couple of people with your creation, that's already a lot!

Here are some questions for the exploration process:

- What new activity would you like to practice?
- How many hours a week do you have available for this new activity?
- How steady is your schedule? So you can add specific days and times.
- If it's not steady, consider activities that you can do by yourself at any time, like painting, reading, or going out.

Please keep in mind that creativity comes from experiences that we have in different levels, mind, heart, and body, so ideally you will try to nurture each of them.

Constancy. This is in the top five of issues that my coachees bring to the sessions. The secret is that most of the time the lack of constancy has to do with having bad plans, or lack of motivation (what you are trying to accomplish is not as important, urgent, or frustrating to you enough).

So from now on, when you find yourself leaving something undone, or in the middle of the project, just ask yourself why you started and if completing it right now is that important, actually, the question would be "How important is it for you to accomplish this from 1 to 10?." The answer will be all you need.

The importance of constancy has to do with the fact that every pro has been an amateur once, so the more we practice what we are doing, the better we will perform. Dedicating time to development is the only way we will move up in the performance ladder. As we start to dominate the discipline or skill, then we will start to feel joy. And there is where the passion is born!

While practicing, you will find yourself having other kinds of challenges. Facing and overcoming them will keep you motivated and will encourage you to keep on learning. This is a key quality for leaders, and as I will review later in chapter 13, we are all leaders at some level, so the first step is to acknowledge that, and to choose the kind of leader you want to be. It can also help to project yourself during the years without having that consistency: How will I find myself in five or ten years if I keep on - complete with the lack of constancy in the activity -? Do you like what you see? If not, you know the answer, create a realistic plan, and create an impact on that future self that you want to be.

Today is the best day to start! If you didn't start by the end of last chapter.

During my grief I put on some weight and I wasn't leaving my house, until my dog, Mila, came into the picture.

At the beginning I would just walk her a couple of blocks. Slowly I started to walk a little more, I would always try to do a little more. One day I ran. By the end of the second month I made it to five km (3.1 miles), which was my goal for the end of the year, and I accomplished it by the end of October.

A year later I still run and I am also going to the gym. I started with a personal trainer online, which is awesome because he adapts the exercises to my preferences. I don't like long workouts, more than forty-five-minutes seems a lot for me, so I found a routine that works for me and I am sticking to it. We all have different ways of accomplishing results, so with this example I am just encouraging you to find your own plan that would work for you, we will review plans in chapter 10. Also, you should know that many other work-out plans didn't work for me in the past, and some other work only for some time.

The shift in my mind came through the understanding that I didn't want a year to go by and find myself in the same situation. Yes, I was grieving, and I gave my body and my mind all the respect they deserve. I also gave them what was good for them, regardless of the effort that it meant for me at that moment, but I was consistently doing it for my future self, trusting in the process. I normally take a minute to thank myself for putting in that time and energy, as well as checking in with myself to be fully aware of how I am feeling. These little moments are part of the motivation I have the next day to do it again, because when I think about my future self, my body and mind are set to get the work out done. I also get dressed in advance, so I am consistent with the decision and I avoid those moments when I am tired or it looks inconvenient. Once I am dressed, there are no excuses. It doesn't matter if I have fifteen, thirty or sixty minutes, all those options are better than nothing.

It took me some time to feel my body strong, and now I can tell you that the benefits of training are further than just physical. I feel healthier. My mind is stronger also. My love for myself too, the acknowledgement that I am loving myself and I do each of these steps caring about myself, make my whole-self feel "next-level" better!

Constancy is developed, and remember to start by checking the plan and the importance of what you are trying to achieve.

Then, project yourself five years from now, with and

without making any changes. Now reconsider the importance of what you are trying to achieve.

If the outcome is important, work on a solid and realistic plan, and find few activities that will create an impact in the long term toward this objective.

Always remember that the sum of little actions creates a big impact. So pick your little-impactful actions and start working to become your best future self!

While constancy has to do with performing an action through time, consistency has to do with performing that action in the same way.

We all know that this doesn't apply to every activity we are performing, but the way I like to apply this concept has to do with our energy, how we show up for our life every day.

Are you setting yourself up for success?

Let's say that you go out partying every single night, and you wake up with a hangover every morning. Are you sure you are doing your best?

This reminds me of Mr. E. There was a session where we were talking about decision making, and the challenge he was facing to stop overthinking some simple choices, such as participating in a tennis tournament.

He started playing last year, so he doesn't consider himself a "great" player, consequently, he struggles to make the decision.

As we were making progress in the session, we started to review how he was setting himself up, was it for success or for failure?

So he ended up discovering that through that whole overthinking process, he would get frustrated, he would lose motivation and willingness to play, so he would make some bad decisions, such as drinking alcohol and not having enough sleep the previous night. Then, he would regret it, he would show up knowing that his chances of winning were little, and of course, he would lose in the first or second round.

I am sharing this story, because Mr. E. can't choose consistency on how he plays, because he is a human being and our performance varies and depends on many factors that we can't control, that are dynamic.

What he can control, and where he can create consistency is in his process. He can consistently set himself up for success, through a routine that would bring his best version into the court. So he started to eat properly, avoid alcohol, have a good amount of sleeping hours, and show up early to spend some time setting up himself in the court.

I would like to encourage you to review your positive habits, such as training, eating healthy, resting, checking in with yourself and making sure that your mind, body, and heart are connected and feeling well. If that wasn't the case, what can you adjust to create a boost in your habits? Think about an activity that would have low effort and high impact.

Here I will leave some questions for you:

- How important is it for me to change this habit/to develop this skill from 1 to 10?
- What would this development give me that I don't have now?
- How would I be in the future if I don't make this change?
- Do I want to keep on being frustrated with this matter a year from now?
- How can I create a small impact? What is the first step to take?

JOURNAL IT

IV

———

VALUES

8

DISCOVERING THE "VALUE"

WHEN TALKING about Values I like to make a distinction between two types of values:

1. Our own value, how much is our worth - The value that I am adding
2. Values as our moral compass

Values:
• The regard that something is held to deserve; the importance, worth, or usefulness of something.
• A person's principles or standards of behavior; one's judgment of what is important in life.

Values may vary according to our culture, that is why it is so important to acknowledge them and to check in with ourselves to make sure that we are aligned and we feel comfortable with corporate values.

I'd like to start with the value that we add.

Many times I heard coachees being motivated to work

for a company based on the value they were adding to the world. And then, many things happen.

Meet Debby, she is in her thirties, she works for a tech company. She's been working there for the past eight years. I've heard her through the sessions talking about how happy she was to work there with all the perks she was receiving, how comfortable she was having a steady job position, how lucky she was to have a great income that was allowing her to afford a certain lifestyle. At that point, she was proud of having that position in that company, she was even presuming of that.

Until last year, when she started feeling some lack of motivation, she couldn't find the reason, so we started to explore and clarify.

At some point she came to the conclusion that she was not aligned with the company values. For all those years she thought she was working for a certain kind of company, and that social media was an amazing way to connect. As I said, she had pride in belonging to that company. She was so sure that her job was important and she was adding value to a greater good.

The problem now is that she is not sure about that greater good or the impact that this company is having, so she doesn't want to be part of that system anymore. The issue she is facing, is that she is not finding another job that would pay her what she is earning, so the choice is to keep on adding value to a cause that she is not supporting anymore, and to be clear, she is against it, or to find another job, add value to another cause that she would support, but won't let her have the lifestyle she is having.

This is a clear example of companies giving team members golden handcuffs. She is not the only one being stuck in a company, there's a difference between being stuck and having a steady job. Most of the time, being stuck looks like lack of motivation, unwillingness to complete the daily tasks, then procrastination, frustration, and desperation.

The observation I have to make is that sometimes being comfortable in a place and being aligned with the values of the company doesn't look like stuckness and it's some kind of steadiness that most of us appreciate. A different situation is when you know that your daily action is having a negative impact on somebody else's life.

Another way things can go:

Gabby is an Architect, she moved to Mexico because she wanted to work in a specific studio, because she supported all the social activities they were doing, on top of having a vanguardist way of using materials and designing.

So she flew there and got the job.

Everything was amazing, the team, the projects, the office, the payment was extremely low, but she was happy to feel compensated through the experience and the opportunity to add value to the place.

One day she came to the session saying that she's been working on extremely luxury projects, that she wasn't there to work on that, and that she didn't see how she was creating an impact on the social constructions she was looking forward to designing.

Through clarification, she came to understand the cycle of the value she was adding. She was not designing those social homes, that was as true as the fact that those homes were designed and financed through the projects she was working on.

Let's go over it. The studio would sell millionaire projects and through the money they were earning, they could afford to build homes for those who were in need.

By understanding this process, she understood that even though her value was not having a direct impact on those social projects, through the value she was adding, the studio was building those homes. Acknowledging which is the grain of sand that we are adding is a key to being aligned with our purpose and intentions.

This is another way of understanding the impact in our actions, directly or indirectly. Being able to analyze the whole picture is important, for the good and for the bad. Being conscious of our choices is important, because we will need to deal with the consequences, and once you realize the impact of your actions, it is hard to go back to a detachment and unconscious state. Also, if we want to live an intentional life, we should choose consciously and intentionally each step.

Moving to values as a moral compass, this looks a little more complex for me.

I'd like to start by acknowledging the fact that the moral compass is affected by many accidents of our life, such as culture, religion, among others.

We will go over those in the next chapter, for now we will stick to an understanding: I will refer to good or bad according to the impact it has on other people. Being responsible only for the choices we are making, leaving on the side the choices others are making.

Through this story I will clarify what I mean.

I met Chad in Miami. We had a casual conversation in a bar. Chad is Argentinian, he was an executive there, until one day he had an anxiety episode that led him to quit his job and start a search for purpose.

He loves surfing, the sea, and a natural and quiet life.

When I met him, he mentioned that his purpose has to do with making surfing more accessible to more people. He wanted to have a surfing school in central America.

What sounded like a contradiction for me, that he was not admitting, was the way he was trying to earn the money to finance the project: he was on his way to California to work in a weed plantation.

So I asked him if that was the only way he could access the money, and he said that it was the best option for him because he would earn it, versus getting a loan that he would have to repay, and also because he had pride on not having to ask for money from anyone.

It is undeniable all the work and the risk he would face through doing it. It was also undeniable that the bigger picture is not nice. This touches a sensitive fiber for me, since one of the people I love most is a weed addict. Nobody told me that, I saw the impact of accepted social drugs in many people's lives.

I am not judging the decision, I am talking about the consistency, the clarity and honesty we have with ourselves and with others when we tell our stories. There is no doubt that Chad means well, there's also no doubt that out of all the options he has, he chose the one that fit him better and adapted his story to the reality he created. Being aligned with our values starts with consistency.

Living a purposeful life has to do with our choices, so we need to make sure we are fully conscious of the impact they have, and if that looks acceptable for us.

Excuses are not allowed, because we can't undo what is done, and there's always another option, there are only a few dead-end roads in life.

What I am also talking about is to be honest with ourselves. Yes, we may also think that this applies to people that have bars, or that sell cigarettes, and to some companies that sell food that is not considered healthy. I'm not judging if those things should or not exist, what I am saying is that we need to be clear about our impact and be fine with it. Part of making conscious choices is to evaluate the risks we are willing to take. Through acknowledging the risks we are taking, we are fully aware of the consequences, so this leads us to the difference between an accident and something that could have been prevented.

Accident:

- a chance and usually sudden event bringing loss or injury.

According to its definition, accidents can't be controlled by us, and have negative consequences. So, an accident couldn't be prevented, if it can be prevented it's not an accident, it's a risk we took and went on a different way than we expected.

I like to think about the moments when we make a decision as a point-zero one. Every time we choose a path over another, we are in a point-zero moment. There's always a point-zero in every relationship, it doesn't matter if the relationship is with a job, a project, drugs, alcohol, people, food, or any other thing we relate with in our life.

At that point-zero we can choose fresh and clear, we are not affected by any feeling or sensation.

Let me say it again in different words, every beginning is an opportunity to make a choice.

That's it! Let's own it!

I'd like to leave out of this reflection all the decisions that are made out of desperation, lack of knowledge or opportunity. Also, my intention is to bring perspective, not judgement.

What I am trying to say is that if I drive when I am drunk and hit something, that wasn't an accident, that was something that could have been prevented. If I start a relationship with a person that I know is married, that's a choice, not an accident, it could have been prevented.

I have to own the fact that I like to exercise self-control, I tend to eat more than I should, and I am a social drinker. As for drugs, I am scared of them, of liking them too much, and I don't like to defy the odds. What if I am part of the 1 percent that goes wrong and something happens to me? I don't know about them, and I dislike being out of control, so I'd rather not try them. Then, I don't date married or committed men, I just dislike the place where that relationship will set me, and I don't want to suffer, so I just don't get involved.

As I am sharing, some of my decisions are motivated out of fear of the consequences, self-love, and the projection of my future self, I think about the person I am and the person I want to be, and I always try to make choices that would get me closer to the person that I want to be. Yes, I said "try", because we are all human beings, we are rational animals, so we still have both components (the rational part and the instinct as animals) and we need to embrace and be at peace with both of them.

I make an effort to make conscious choices, it's an exercise, it's committing to myself, I'm not saying it's easy or that I manage them perfectly, I am saying that it is possible if we have the intention.

And of course, I have some questions:

- What were those accidents in your life that could have been prevented?
- How would you prevent the next preventable accident?
- How are you making conscious and impactful choices for your wellbeing?
- What thought or feeling would help you to make your choices easier?

Going back to Values, here's my story that mixes a little bit of both meanings:

When I came to the US, we bought a franchise with my sister. We picked the company; it is a cleaning company. Corporate office has some campaigns that helped us create a social impact in the neighborhood, and we liked that. As far as the company itself, I have to admit that other than the fact that we used eco-friendly products, I wasn't conscious about other impacts. So this is what I had about the part of creating values.

Then, as for the moral compass, we were aligned, there was nothing wrong with the corporate office and the people that were working there, the relationship was professional and we believed in the system that apparently was already working in the US.

Time started to go by with us managing the business, and we started noticing that none of south Florida new offices were picking up. We were all growing, but not as much as we were supposed to be.

At the beginning of the issue, we were all blamed for not managing the business as it was supposed to, we were all reviewing our methods, processes, everything! We are all accomplished people, that has always kept my attention. I know we were operating in a new country, but it couldn't be a coincidence that we were all failing.

Eventually we found out that the marketing system was not working well, but we had to pay for it anyway because of the contract. It was extremely inefficient.

Years went by. We were managing a bigger business, dealing with a lot of responsibilities and stressing situations. We reached 325 regular customers and a team of more than twenty people. But those marketing expenses were killing us. For many years those expenses were preventing my sister and me to afford a manager's minimum wage. We were struggling to pay our personal expenses; we were extremely stressed. I started to feel it in my body, and my mind. There were times that I would be driving and I would think "The only way of getting out of this is if I crash my car and go to the hospital for a couple of days 'to rest'." It is so crazy just to think about that. I'm not talking about suicidal thoughts, I am talking about the need to slow down, the desperation of giving 100 percent all the time and being in an unfair situation that wasn't leading to an immediate solution.

I can't deal with unfairness, and that's my own problem, I know, still, I'd rather be fair!

All south Florida owners manifested this problem, we had the experience and the tools to prove what we were saying. It was not only about the fact that we were all struggling to make a "decent" living, but it was also about an unhealthy business. So we had a call with the COO where she suggested we keep on sending the brochures anyway, because we still needed to pay for that amount to the corporate office. To put this clearly, she was saying that we had to keep on spending the money, just because of the contract, even though she knew and admitted that the money we were spending was not bringing business to us.

That was a deal breaker for me. I left my office a little more than a year after that, I couldn't take it anymore. This situation plus my feeling that this project had taken so many precious moments. I missed so many times for being tired, stressed, and that was priceless. I gave everything I had, and I can say that the business was successful from the perspective that before the pandemic we've been for a couple of months making a decent amount of money, and I think that my feeling of accomplishment let me go without any regret. I don't feel like a failure, I feel that I've been in that business for as long as we needed to get our heads out of the water. But that money was meaningless for me, because I already had this feeling in my chest that I wasn't being treated and respected as the kind of person I am. I have pride in saying that I am not that kind of business person, and as a business person, I am a person doing business.

My thought is, if "business is business," then "business is business"?

The question is: Where is the limit?

When I communicated to the Operations Representative that I was leaving the office, he said something like "My only concern is How are you going to deal with this failure?"

Failure? Or can we call it integrity, bravery, or partnership commitment to move forward in the best way we could?

My sister and I decided that she would stay in the company and I would leave. I was going to leave regardless of whether she wanted to stay or not. She decided to stay, this doesn't mean that she is fine with the way they are doing business, this only means that she can deal with it in a different way, and she finds a purpose through the business in other ways that I couldn't.

We both fully supported each other in the paths we were taking.

She witnessed how bad that company had been for me, how much I suffered for not receiving answers, for being blamed and underestimated. For trying to do business under unfair conditions that were clear and at the same time consistently denied or overlooked. I even wondered if I would have been treated the same way if I had been an American.

I have no regrets; it was an amazing chapter of my life that gave me many opportunities at different levels. The most important thing for me is that I grew closer to my sister, I learned so much from her that I lost count of all those things. I am extremely proud of the decision she made and how she is navigating the pandemic. Also, about the person she became through this experience. I love you Fi, I will be forever thankful for the opportunity we had to share all that time together and even though that chapter was hard, the one we are writing now is much better thanks to the past one.

I'm sharing this because I have many reflections to make:

- What does failure mean?
- What is the price that we pay for staying in a place that is not good for us?
- What kind of business person are you?
- What kind of business person do you want to be?
- Why do we associate endings to failure?
- How do we choose to live our life?
- When staying is the brave decision: Why are you choosing to stay? Just stick to that reason and move forward

According to this chapter, we can appreciate how impactful the concept of value is, and how we can find it in different ways. This is why I invite you to think about your values, the value you are adding, the extra value you could add, to define your values as in your moral compass, to reflect about those point-zero moments you had, and the choices you made, would you make the same choice if you knew how it would end up? What would you do in the next point-zero you face? Take some time to think about those "accidents" that could have been prevented, and to own those "accidents" that even though could have been prevented you chose not to.

I don't think that there's anything good or bad about the way we choose to live our lives, I am saying that the sooner we take responsibility and own our decisions, the better, because we would be in peace and aligned with ourselves, and that's the only thing that matters!

As per our core values, our moral compass, here are some questions that may help you identify them:

- Which are the core values that lead your life?
- How much are you honoring them in each area of your life?
- What could you do to be more aligned with your own truth?
- How are you adding value to a bigger cause through your daily work?
- How could you add more value to the people around you in each area of your life?

9

I AM WORTHY

NORMAL:

- That serves as a norm or rule.
- That it conforms to a certain norm or habitual or current characteristics, without exceeding or lacking.

Personally, I think we can talk about norms and rules when we refer to basic ethical parameters (and even those are debatable according to religions and cultures), however, I think that we should pay more attention to how we express ourselves, because we do not know the connotation that that may have in others.

I leave some questions for reflection:

- What does it mean to be normal in 2021?
- Who wants to be normal? Possibly the one who suffered being himself; winged as "abnormal" (different from the rule)

Speaking with my roommate, I told him that I feel normal with him, that many times I suffered from not feeling normal. To which he replied, "who wants to be normal?" And I kept thinking, because in reality I did not mind being normal, I was fine being different, while I was in a relationship, but when I was single it was difficult for me. I find it difficult to love and accept myself without fitting into social standards and without complying with social mandates. Socially, we see a woman separated, single, or strong, entrepreneurial or whatever she does not fit into marriage with children and it is automatically assumed that the woman is of a certain shape, and that shape has negative connotations.

So, recapping, it didn't bother me to be different as long as I kept certain socially accepted forms. But now that I separate and rethink this situation, I realize that it is good to be different, it is as good to be different as to respond to the norm, it is good what makes each of us happy, and to accept that not all of us are happy in the same way, and that our task is to find what makes us happy.

I was also surprised how a man who does not fit social standards is overrated, and as a woman she is rather rare.

When talking to him I realized that it all depends on who you hang out with. He has a life with a different mental openness regarding mandates, and in that sense I am learning that what I consider normal (norm), is what I saw when I grew up, is what I experience according to my environment, but in reality, the norm is what each one has seen and how each one has grown.

Religion.

I was born in a Catholic family. I went to a Catholic school and University.

For my family religion is important.

Religion:

- a particular system of faith and worship – Oxford dictionaries

If I'm getting this right, religion is the shape of spirituality, as a system, it is a sum of organized practices that help all of us to express our faith in the same way.

Many years ago, I was going through a bad moment and a friend of mine invited me to go to a spiritual retreat.

It was a mind-blowing experience for me, I was completely out of my comfort zone, and I was not sure about what I would discover.

I have to admit that it was way more than what I expected. I heard many things completely different than what I grew up believing. It seemed to me that it was a new church, an updated or modernized church.

What is important for me to share is that I truly understood what some things were about. I have to say also that it depends on the priest or nuns you are talking to, but the truth is that even though I am considered a sinner, I sleep in peace at night.

Let's see, sex before marriage. Some of us are sinners in that one. The explanation I received is that the expectation for the church is that you are in a situation where you are fully respected, loved or cared for, with consent, and having a deep connection that would lead to a healthy and loving moment.

Looking around I understand that the church is against you hurting your mind, body, and soul through taking the risk of having a bad experience that can come from a "casual" encounter, being "casual" out of marriage. Again, this is a way of setting a clear standard or rule for a certain time period.

This is pretty different than literally not having sex until you are married. Also, from my perspective, this is an area where self-love and respect are especially important.

I am also guilty of getting married legally and not in the church, so a priest told me that unless I got married I couldn't commune anymore. And that's fine! There are rules, and it's fine for me to stick to them, but there's a difference between having a heavy conscience about something we did that is wrong, and it is causing harm, and something that is not affecting anyone else except for me and my husband (ex-husband now). So yes, I will become a divorced woman, I may melt the next time I get in a church, but I know that I did it for love, that circumstances changed but I meant well, and I didn't hurt anyone!

So, how do we align our values to religion?

From my perspective, I strongly respect religion, and I practice it, I pray and every now and then I go to church, it's just that I am living my life according to my reality. Yes, I could have chosen to stay in a marriage that was not working at 32. However, it is hard for me to believe that God wants that for me. I am not saying that we should be happy at whatever cost, I am saying that as long as we are not making any harm to others or ourselves, we should be free to live our lives, understanding that as human beings the need of spirituality is within us, and the religion is the organization of those spiritual ideas, so we can still be spiritual people and practice according to the religion we learned, without being limited in our elections by it.

Almost every religion has rules that at some point may seem limiting, it's just that those rules are better explained and adapted to this era. Only God is perfect, and he understands, he is compassionate. We are human beings, what matters is that we live a life with kindness in our hearts and balance in our decisions.

Loving and respecting ourselves should be the most

important item, as well as loving and respecting each other. Again, as long as I do that, I feel I am not guilty or a sinner, and by simplifying it, and understanding the context, I know I make choices for myself that are aligned with most religions.

When I went to New Orleans, I learned that Voodoo is a religion. It is comes from Africa, and people of African descent practiced it while pretending they were practicing Catholicism, which was the imposed religion. There were so many similarities between both religions that it was easy for them to practice "Catholicism." This is because it combines Roman Catholicism with West African spiritual traditions. (I admit that both religions are much more complex than that, but I do not want to get too sidetracked in religious study.) One important detail to point out is that Voodoo lacks centralized, standardized doctrines that govern practice. For instance, even though there is a sense of crime

What I am trying to say, is that it is important to have a spiritual practice, as I said, religion is the organization of those ideas and practices, but at the end of the day, it doesn't matter what church do you go to, what religion you are practicing, or the name of your God, for me there's only one and we can find it everywhere. I normally don't talk or discuss religion because for me it's about the positive aspects of it, the comfort that it brings me to have faith and surrender, knowing that there's a greater good, a purpose, and that everything happens for a reason, and I don't complain about other messages that are interpreted by human beings, through their own filters, because I am a human being and I can still make my own interpretations, as well as you can.

Each religion has different rules and understandings, living in a global world I consider it particularly important to reflect on this, we may be from one place living in another, working for a company whose culture belongs to another part of the world, so, one more time, taking a moment to reflect on our behaviors and values, and staying aligned and honoring them in the way we consciously choose, seems a key to have peace of mind and fulfilment, as well as performing better on each area of our lives.

Boundaries.

When talking about boundaries, well, that's a hard topic for me, it's funny how as I was reading a book I thought that my boundaries were fine, until I had a conversation with one of my sisters and she reminded me of situations where there was a complete lack of boundaries in the family.

There was no harm, let's say that I went on vacation with my friends, and my brother went to the same place with his friends, and one morning my parents with my younger siblings showed up at the hotel where we were staying. At that moment we had fun, it seemed so cool that they came to share the moment with us, but at the same time, there's another perspective, there was such a lack of boundaries that they showed up unexpectedly in the middle of our vacation with friends.

There was this other time when one of my sisters was in Europe and my mother reorganized her closet, my other sister told my mom that she didn't want that, that she wouldn't like that "surprise," so my mother said that it was fine, she was not going to do it for her, but she didn't see how it was crossing a privacy line.

Let's not get stuck in these two examples, please understand that these are only two moments that I clearly remember that there were no boundaries.

I can add the fact that I've been unintentionally bullied most of my life. Those were jokes, but I internalized them and they became insecurities and doubts. It has to do with me, not with my siblings or their friends, because I understand that we were laughing, it's just that I was unable to speak and say that it was not fine for me, because I knew that nobody meant bad. In addition to what I said at the beginning of the book, I used to try to belong.

It wasn't until last year that I finally said that I didn't have to keep on putting up with all those jokes, that they were not funny for me, and that I needed them to stop with that. They totally understood, and apologized. They thought it was a game and never imagined that those comments were hurting me, the problem was my difficulty in setting boundaries, and expressing myself. That was a game, for sure, but it was hurting me, and I was part of it also, because I felt it was funny, until it wasn't.

What is crazy is that I almost skipped the "Boundaries" chapter of the book that I was reading. I am so sensitive that I couldn't face the fact that my parents, or my siblings are anything less than loving and amazing. And that's how they are, as well as human beings, as I am also, and those things that affected me, may or may not have affected others in the same way.

Setting boundaries is important because it has to do with communicating what we like and what we don't, what we want and what we don't. It requires self-knowledge and self-love. It's also about owning your decisions according to your own compass, versus the family or social compass. I'm talking about maturity, independence, and individuality. Facing the fact that your parents (and any other family member or friend) may have lived their lives in a different way than you, and that the rules and decisions that they made were in a different context and from their own beliefs. We are all entitled to live our own lives as we choose to. Making your own choices may be a challenge for people like me, but it is worth it! I promise!

It may be a coincidence or a God-incidence, but I signed the contract to write this book on July 9th, Argentina's independence day. It seems to me that I declared my own independence that same day!

So here's the deal. Some of us come from places were people identify themselves in groups, it gives us a sense of belonging, and also, it takes from us part of our uniqueness, let me explain: "We eat pasta with cheese because we are Italians", "We are Di Fabio, so we are A,B,C…" As I said, those expressions take part of our differences and make a blend, so instead of being different colors, we all become a big amount of brown paint.

I've been living up to those false senses of belonging my whole life. I've been ignoring myself, I even thought I was not normal.

With all this being said, I strongly encourage you to go deep inside yourself and double check those limits that you are setting for the people around you. Those people could be your parents, siblings, grandparents, friends, partner, whoever is not giving you the respect in terms of privacy and space for decisions, just know that you can speak and that is relieving, it is worthy, you are worthy of having those boundaries in your life.

For me one of the first steps on setting boundaries is to learn how to say "no." It can be just "no" or it can also be a polite and clear expression that means "no." However you feel more comfortable.

Just know that having a full schedule eventually will detach your body from your mind. We learn how to ignore the feelings of tiredness, the joy, the sadness.

With boundaries in place, we can more easily feel our body and through that connection choose which activities we prefer to do, and when it is time to say no.

Boundaries also help us to feel more comfortable when sharing our feelings and emotions, and as we feel emotionally safe, we share our thoughts, opinions, and beliefs with others. We also learn who and when we want to share those feelings.

- Have you ever felt that you were telling something personal to someone random?
- How do you feel about expressing your thoughts, ideas, and beliefs?
- How easy is it for you to say "no" or set a limit from 1 to 10?

Fears

Definition: an unpleasant emotion caused by the belief that someone or something is dangerous, likely to cause pain, or a threat.

Many times in my life I faced situations that were scary for me, so I will share what I learned from them.

As the definition established, it is an unpleasant emotion. When talking about emotions, there is not a real way to measure it. It is legit, if you're feeling it, it is happening, so here's the deal:

First scenario: If a lion crosses the door of the room where you are sitting right now, you will be scared. There is real danger, the lion can definitely eat you, and won't ask for permission, and you won't be able to stop it (unless you have a gun or something, but let's say that you don't have it).

Second scenario: a cockroach crosses the door of the room where you are right now, you will be scared (you can change cockroach for any other insect that scares you). There is no real danger, it couldn't hurt you even if it wanted to.

So, in both situations we were scared, and as I said, it is legit, but we both can agree on the fact that there was no danger in the second scenario, right?

Well, when I am scared of something I try to think if I am facing a lion or a cockroach, and by identifying it, I am already working on the facts that there are and would support that identification.

Then, I may work in my head or even write down a list consistently answering this question: "what happens if this goes wrong?" Eventually I come to a point where the answer is "nothing," and of course, a list of outcomes and possible solutions.

Most of the time, all those things never happen, it all goes in the way it should, and whatever that way it is, I trust that I will always find a way to move forward. I now know that life will always give me the tools and resources I need on each moment to move forward through challenges and hard times.

Now think about yourself, think about a moment in your life when something unexpected happened.

Once you identify that moment, try to make a path from that moment to today, and how you were able to go through the situation, how you grew as a result from it. Think about how impacted your life and all the great things that came as a consequence.

After walking through that thought, I am confident that now you also know and trust that you can solve whatever life throws at you. There will be harder moments than others, even moments where you would say "I'm not seeing how I will get out of this." I've been there, many times, and I can tell you without any doubt that you have what it takes to deal with your own life.

Ok, that's for difficult moments. Now, let's move to moments where there were two options, you had a Plan A and a Plan B, and you wanted it to be Plan A, but for any reason, fate, you ended up doing Plan B.

The exercise is the same, think about all the great things that happened as a result of that single moment, think about all the ways that you evolved as a consequence of that situation, and how it impacted your life.

How we deal with those events is up to us. At this point we already know that. So, for me it has to do with identifying the opportunity in each event, as well as adding a little extra of our uniqueness. What is the opportunity here? How can I take this opportunity to the next level?

For me it is important to always have clear intentions. If we send to the Universe messages from fear or negativity, and unclear, things will unfold in a different way than what we thought we expected.

I was looking for an apartment, I wanted to move in September, I set a budget and priorities. I've been looking since April, but doing nothing because I wasn't ready to move forward. That was creating some anxiety, but I was focused on the certainty that there was an apartment that was meant to be for me. In August I started looking and was ready to move forward, and I went to see one that had all the priorities and budget. I rented it without even walking through, the only issue was that the moving date is in November. I took this event as an opportunity on different levels, and I can confirm that it is great for my healing and development path.

In conclusion, it's all about our mindset. Identifying those situations that may cause us fear and turn them into opportunities through love and faith is what will make the difference.

Based on this, my thought is that we can all change our limiting beliefs or expressions. I didn't dare to dream about writing a book because "I am a numbers person" I used to identify myself with an excel spreadsheet. I am complex, I like some structure, I understand numbers pretty well, and I like functionality more than aesthetic. Eventually, I changed that thought. When I moved to the US with my sister, it challenged many of these beliefs, because to build a business from scratch requires a different skill set than the one I was used to practicing in Argentina, while managing a steady business. I had the opportunity to learn from her flexibility, from the importance of aesthetics as well as functionality, I had to adapt, and at the end of the day, those expressions were just limiting me.

The good news is that we can all change, and the change comes from inside.

This has to do with the stories we tell ourselves. Those stories are typically created in our childhood, and we keep repeating them and consequently believing them. So from here we need to understand the importance of updating these stories.

As a child, I used to be shy. I wasn't sympathetic because I had insecurities and I was shy. I grew up saying that, however, the truth is that I worked a lot on that, and I became a totally different person. I am an easy going and approachable person, and I had to update my story for me to feel myself.

The same happens with our core beliefs, for instance, I grew up hearing that I was lazy. However, the truth is that I didn't care to participate in certain activities, mostly because most of the people around me were better than me at those activities. I am talking about going to my grandparents' home and having to participate in regular household chores. So, I'd rather don't do them, than to be compared or criticized. I still prefer not to do them, but as I am not compared or criticized, I do those chores and I thank myself for whatever I managed to do.

Of course, I realized this over time, but somewhere in my head I could hear those words. I became a workaholic. For many years I asked myself "When am I going to be enough for myself?" "Who am I trying to impress?" "What do I have to prove?."

I used to challenge myself, to acknowledge the difficulty, and then, after the accomplishment I would say "If I could do it, it was not that difficult."

Studying coaching was the ultimate way I challenged myself. I was working, and I enrolled in the UM, classes were by phone in English (this used to be one of my biggest insecurities), and I had to take a couple of exams and coach in front of my classmates.

It was definitely challenging for me. I told myself that if I could do it I would know that that was it, I would stop challenging myself from a lacking perspective, I would keep on challenging myself because it also motivates me.

And then, the day came, I finished, I still had to sit for an exam, but I had made it, and again, I wasn't feeling that fulfilment, it didn't feel like the ultimate accomplishment.

Through practicing self-love, and getting to appreciate myself better, and being more realistic with the fears, challenges, and difficulties, I got to a moment where I made it happen. It was when I sat for the last coaching exam, it was a multiple choice, and I've always struggled with them. It was so hard for me, I pushed myself along the exam, I had to refocus many times, and when I passed, it was like the day I got my degree, I felt it in my body! The difference is that this time, I thought "this is it! I can and I am making it happen, I am enough for myself!." It was the acknowledgement that coaching became a lifestyle in which I consistently overcame challenges to get to this final result.

I was feeling so unstoppable that I decided to write this book!

JOURNAL IT

V

GOALS

10

THE SET UP

Goals:
• Daily action
• The object of a person's ambition or effort; an aim or desired result.

ACCORDING TO THE DEFINITION, to have a goal we need to have the intention to achieve the result, as well as being willing to make the effort.

I will also use this moment as an opportunity to define ambition, and make sure that we take it in a positive way:

Ambition:
• A strong desire to do or to achieve something, typically requiring determination and hard work

I love this definition, and I don't find anything wrong about it. A lot of times my coachees say, "It's not that I am ambitious," but yes, it is about it. There's nothing wrong with being determined, and to work hard for what we want to achieve. I am ambitious, and I hope you are also.

Now we can go back to goals, as we said before, the exploration of new tasks and activities, and then the practice, will lead us to our passion, and consequently, in the choices of those actions, we will live a purposeful life.

When we talk about goals, we talk about S.M.A.R.T. goals: Specific, Measurable, Achievable, Realistic, and Timely.

The importance of setting accurate goals is to make them intentional. Choose goals that will make an impact on your life purpose, on a daily, weekly, and monthly basis. This way you can create habits, and by taking every choice as an opportunity you will create a fulfilling lifestyle.

I see GOALS as the organization of your hard work, as well as the steps that will let you create your desired lifestyle, while developing yourself to become your best version

In this chapter it is my intention that you get all the tools that you need to create a good plan. As I said before, I've seen countless times how making a bad plan prevents people from reaching their goals.

When we talk about GOALS, we talk about daily action. For me it is the glue for all the other components. We've been going through the importance of making intentional choices, through the goals and a customized, sustainable plan, we set ourselves up for success.

The difference between a goal and a plan is that the goal is the destination, the plan is how we will get there, that's why both parts have the same importance to get where we want to be. We can't go to a specific place if we don't know where we are going, and we can't get there either if we don't know how. We will go over goals and plans in this chapter.

Now that we are ready to create an impact, the next step is to define where we are right now? This is a pretty open question, we can relate it to each area of your life, not only the one that we are trying to work in.

Here are some questions that will apply to many different areas and will help you create the first picture:

- What is the issue?
- How is it affecting my professional and personal life?
- Why is it important for me to overcome this now?
- How will my personal and professional life be different if I resolve this issue?
- What will overcoming this issue give me that I don't have right now?

These are just some of the questions that you can ask yourself, here's an example of another coachee, who was struggling to set boundaries.

Setting boundaries at work was the challenge she was facing. It was causing overworking, that means that she needed to stay later to complete the extra work she agreed on doing, but disliked doing it, and it was not part of her job description. This was also causing frustration, and it was impacting her personal life, because she ended up being so tired that most of the days she skipped training, and got home so frustrated that didn't want to go out with her friends, or if she did, she tended to complain about her job. Some other days when she managed to work out late, she would end up ordering food because she didn't have time to cook or buy groceries.

It was important for her to address this because she needed a radical change and she was trying to focus on getting the management of a new area, so she needed to be laser-focused on her priorities and perform the tasks that would take her to the next position.

As a consequence of this change, she would get the position she wanted, she would earn more money, challenge herself in different ways, she would have more responsibilities as well as more flexibility.

Overcoming this issue would give her a more balanced life, she would be able to leave the office when she is done with her tasks, this will let her exercise more, be more organized with groceries, plans with friends, and most importantly, she won't be frustrated about the feeling of being stuck doing something that is not her responsibility, and won't give her any credits.

As we can see, it looks pretty simple the issue or challenge she is facing, but through answering the questions we get to understand better the whole context and impact. Just appreciate how a small action, on a regular basis can create such a big impact.

Once we have the picture of where we are right now, we need to set the picture of where we want to go:

- How would it be if it was perfect? How do you imagine it being fantastic?

Going back to the example:

If her situation was perfect, she would be able to tell Marcia that she won't do her the favor of taking care of any of her tasks. She would tell her boss that she will take care the following day of the assignment she is giving her five-minutes before she leaves, instead of keeping on working at home. Avoid taking care of projects that don't belong to her area. She would stop accepting projects that her team members send her, and for which she doesn't get the credit. She will stop answering working calls on random hours. She would leave work in a good mood, ready for the next activity she wants to do, she would be enthusiastic and full of energy, she loves training and going out with friends.

The next step is to compare that fantastic picture with reality. It's pretty obvious in this situation what adjustments are needed.

The adjustments are pretty clear:

- Stop answering the phone in random hours
- Leave the office on time and keep on working tomorrow, unless there's an emergency
- Saying "no" to Marcia and other team members, and being more organized between the urgent and important tasks

Now is time to set the GOAL:

For us to set goals properly, we will do it through SMART method:

SMART:

- Specific (simple, sensible, significant): Set boundaries
- Measurable (meaningful, motivating): She will practice setting one limit every day.
- Achievable (agreed, attainable): It's a transition, it will be uncomfortable, but she can commit to do it. Once a day!
- Relevant (reasonable, realistic, and resourced, results-based): By doing it every day she will be creating a habit, these are little steps that will add on.
- Time bound (time-based, time limited, time/cost limited, timely, time-sensitive): She will do it for two weeks, then we will check in and define her next step.

So, here we have a plan. If she wanted to set all boundaries at once, every time she has the opportunity a day, she would end up being exhausted and stressed, because her habit is to accept what others are doing. Most people fall into immediate results ignoring the impact of baby steps, they try to go from 0 to 100 in three seconds. Then, they end up not making it, abandoning the goal, being frustrated, demotivated and what is even worse, they have the belief that they failed, because they genuinely tried, it's just that they didn't regulate the energy and the impact properly.

To help you with this I will add here two matrices that I love using, they are simple and they help us track energy and impact, as well as setting priorities, urgent versus important.

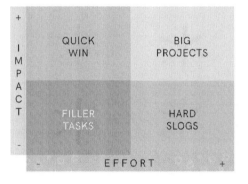

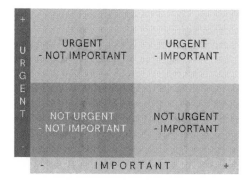

About the first one, there are a couple of things to take into consideration. First of all, it is important to work around effort and impact, because sometimes we choose the hardest and most difficult option. For instance, let's say that we want to have a barbecue in the backyard, so we are working with two options, bringing a container, or building it ourselves with wood. When considering effort we need to take into account all the resources that we need to put in (money, time, energy, raw material, human resources), the knowledge that we have versus the knowledge that we need, among other indicators.

Then, we move to impact, we need to consider the result we are expecting, time frame to get to the result. We are considering that I am making the decision and I don't have the knowledge or strength to build the barbecue. So, the smartest decision will be to bring a container, it will take way less amount of decisions, actions, and with my knowledge I know I can manage to make it happen. However, trying to build that whole barbecue would be setting myself up for failure.

What I am trying to show you is that we need to make simple decisions and set realistic goals. There's a lot of indicators when considering effort and impact, and the most important measurement is the chance that we have to make it happen.

Secondly, and analyzing each part of the matrix, I always try to stay in the "quick wins." What is key for me is to break down the big projects in a way that I end up having simple and small tasks. This way I can check and appreciate the progress. In my experience, almost everyone is motivated through action. Action brings more action. A coachee said to herself and I will share it with you: "DO, lazily, but DO!"

Sometimes we get caught up with big projects and we avoid facing them because we don't know where to start, we feel overwhelmed.

Let's set an example, if I am trying to organize my finances, it may sound like a lot. However, when I break it down it will look easier and achievable:

- Define the income
- Frequency or time of the month that we receive it
- Make a list of the credit cards
- Identify the closing dates and payment days
- Make a list of the prioritized expenses, such as rent/mortgage, utilities, car expenses, vet, food, gym, hairdresser, etc. (everything that is a priority for you)
- Make a list of other expenses, such as going out, ordering food, shoes, clothes, etc. (everything you like doing extra but is expendable)
- Organize all the information: + Income - prioritized expenses = gross amount available. Then: + Gross amount available - other expenses = net amount available.

Of course we want the net amount available to be positive. I am not considering savings here, or cash, and many other things, but again, this is an example to show that through breaking big projects down, you will stay performing quick wins, since none of these tasks will take you more than twenty minutes. This can be done with every single big project, and through making a list you can choose the task you want to complete according to your mood. Who doesn't have twenty minutes a day? If your finances are a priority, you will find that time, and over a whole week you will have a clear picture of your economic position.

We would try to avoid performing hard slogs, even though we can still break them down to make them quick wins.

As for the filler tasks, those are tasks that you can perform in a couple of minutes in between tasks, before a break or so, they are not important, but we still need to make them happen.

Moving to the second matrix, identifying what is urgent and important will help us to set our priorities. I always try to stay performing important tasks, rather than "urgent and important" tasks.

"Important" tasks not resolved on time, become "urgent and important," and the problem is that when it becomes urgent, we can't choose the best time for us to do it, we need to take care of it immediately, as a priority, even when we had a different plan for the day. So, working with a good plan, setting priorities, and making things happen ahead of time is what will let us increase our performance and productivity.

Those tasks that aren't urgent or important, shouldn't be done, at all. As for the urgent and not important, I'd encourage you to delegate them.

How do we delegate?

When delegating I like doing it through these tips:

- Explain the importance of the task well done
- What is the expected outcome?
- Provide with written instructions while showing the person how to perform
- Give the person a range of decisions to make, and when she should contact you to make a decision
- Mention the consequences for the company and the team if the task is not properly done
- Ask for doubts or questions
- Make the person execute it
- Teach the person how to control herself when she is done with the task
- Have a simple method to control the result for yourself

It may look like a lot, but I promise, it is simple. Just make sure that you are setting the other person up for success. If you think about everything that you know about the task, and how you would be succeeding at performing it, then it becomes even simpler.

This is not the only way of doing it, and many people may feel uncomfortable explaining so much or giving too much detail. For me, it is how I like to do it, the better they understand the process, the better they perform, and the less amount of calls I receive for simple issues. They will communicate when there's a solution, but I give my team members a range to make decisions. That shows trust and empowers them. And also, through participating, they may bring new ideas.

Most of my coachees are entrepreneurs. Today I was coaching Carola and she was telling me how important it was for her to acknowledge that being a business owner is a solitary path. She struggles to share her daily challenges, issues, and frustrations, and she normally feels alone and that nobody understands her.

If you are feeling the same way, reach out for help, you can always meet people at networking chapters, co-working spaces, entrepreneurship groups, and more. Just know that you don't need to be alone, and that there are many other people in the same situation that you are, facing the same challenges. So keep up the good work and reach out for your entrepreneurial community!

Going back to the benefits of goal setting, through them we can create new habits.

Habit:
• a settled or regular tendency or practice, especially one that is hard to give up.

Why is this important now if we already saw it in chapter 6?

Because for us to create a new habit, we need to have the objective of making it happen. Through goal setting, and the understanding that, according to Nicole LePera in "how to do the work," "we operate only 5 percent of the day in a conscious state," now, we will be able to go deeper on habit development.

To clarify, we only respond consciously 5 percent of the time. The other 95 percent of the time, we are only reacting unconsciously. So, to create a new habit, we need to use that 5 percent of focus that we have, and then slowly transform the 95 percent of the time that we spend reacting with our unconscious part.

Let's review an example to use the 5 percent consciousness to develop good habits that we will incorporate in the 95 percent of the unconscious.

I have a coachee that is always complaining about everything. He lives his life in a bad mood, he always sees the half of the glass that is empty, and he complains. His goal was to change that, so as in many other opportunities, he started by having a glass of water in the morning. This will give him consistency, and a couple of minutes to set his mood in positive and look through that glass.

He started to try different morning routines that would set him in a good mood. He would try to see the good and the opportunity on challenges and issues. He created a routine to go back to his good mood, just little steps, a song, a little walk around the block.

Over a month he was another person. Literally. He changed his energy so much that things started to go better, even people started to notice it. Now he is still practicing those things, but what is important, is that he doesn't have to do it on purpose, he managed to change his habit.

The more we practice, the more we keep it in mind. According to the National Science Foundation, 80 percent of the thoughts we have per day are negative and 95 percent are repetitive thoughts. If we repeat those negative thoughts, we think negative way more than we think positive thoughts.

So, if we control our thoughts, and make sure we have more positive thoughts, and we have the habit of seeing things through love, opportunities, and faith lenses, we will end up repeating more positive thoughts than negative, and that would make a huge difference.

Getting all the ideas together, we have 5 percent of focus to change the 95 percent of reactions that we do unconsciously. And of all that 100 percent of thoughts that we have on a daily basis, 95 percent are repetitive thoughts. So, we better start appreciating that 5 percent that is letting us change our thought process and lets start creating new, positive, enthusiastic thoughts and habits, to have a better life!

With all this being said, and considering that a lot of

people struggle with working their plans, changing their behaviors, and developing their habits, please take this information as one of the keys to take into account:

- We can't make a twenty-five-hour plan, every day has only twenty-four hours, and when we learn how to use them, they are more than enough.
- We can't process more changes than the amount of concentration we have available to focus and execute them, so choose baby steps, take it easy and be nice to yourself.
- Make sure that you are creating a realistic and achievable plan. It is better to be an achiever and feel motivated, than overplanning and being frustrated and feeling like a failure.

Failure

- lack of success

Success:

- the accomplishment of an aim or purpose

It seems pretty clear to me that failure is subjective, and that success is objective. Failure depends on success. Then, success depends on achieving certain goals or outcomes. We are in charge of defining those goals, outcomes, targets, or any other way you want to call it. Are you seeing it already?

As we are the only responsible for defining what success means and looks like for us, then, we are fully responsible for becoming successful or to fail. This means that the perspective on success and failure changes. What I am trying to point out here is that the concept itself is up to us, and that we may be successful regardless of the goal we achieved. It's a mindset.

Let's say that I am trying to lose weight, so I change my diet and I start going to the gym. After a couple of months, my weight is exactly the same, but the shape of my body changed. I have a lot more muscle, I am eating healthier, I am resting better, I even have a better mood.

This may seem like a failure, because the initial goal was to lose weight. However, we can also consider it a success, since what I am getting are a lot of other benefits, regardless of the weight.

Understanding that accepting and being grateful for other outcomes or resources that life is giving us, is a choice. You can choose to see the opportunity, and be grateful for it, or you can choose to get angry, frustrated, and stubborn about an outcome that many times is not even the best.

In a coaching session with Mr. E., he discovered that his difficulty to adapt to these new outcomes, was also a difficulty he has to adapt to new life events, or changes in plans. He was consistently talking about failure, and his fear of trying and not making it happen. This fear is limiting him to unleash his full potential. How? Here is the process: His mother has always been very demanding. This created a fear of not being successful, so as a defense mechanism, he self-boycott through not giving his 100percent. Through doing this, when he doesn't reach excellence he has the excuse of having room to do better, of having more to give. Over time, this becomes a comfort zone, a known dynamic, we already know what will happen, we are used to it, and we avoid the discomfort of giving our 100percent and being vulnerable, and not being the best.

This is the comfort zone, until it becomes the uncomfort zone. It isn't until we are uncomfortable and frustrated enough that we look for a change.

With this being said, I can only add the fact that life is dynamic, so it's important to be able to adapt, and how worthy it is to work in our mindset.

I encourage you to double check:

- How are you adapting to dynamic situations?
- How are you talking to yourself?
- What kind of mindset do you have?
- What kind of mindset would you like to have?
- How will you get to that desired mindset?
- Which limiting stories should you look at to make that happen?
- How uncomfortable are you in your comfort zone from 1 to 10?

ACCEPTING WITH HUMBLENESS WHAT LIFE IS GIVING US AND having a winning attitude and mindset will take you further. This includes seeing the opportunities in unexpected outcomes.

One more thing, I am a strong believer that life, or God, or the universe, won't put us through any pain or suffering if it is not with a greater purpose. So, we can manage our success through our thoughts and perspectives, and we can also do it through faith, surrendering to our greater purpose.

What happens when we can't find a way out of a situation?

It may seem like a complete failure. Yes, I know what I said before, but it is also true that sometimes we find ourselves overwhelmed and desperate, and we don't find the way out. All seems to be closed roads. The solutions look huge compared to what we are capable of managing.

The problem we face when we are not able to find a way

out of a situation, is that we stop trying. And by stopping taking action we get into a hopeless state, we get tired, more frustrated, and we just go around being miserable and complaining. That belief that there's no way out becomes our feeling, and then it turns into our behavior.

At this point everything is aligned to be gray. Nothing is colorful anymore, your mind, your heart, your behavior, and also your body are in a permanent state of negativity.

I would like to define problem, so we have a good understanding of what we are talking about:

Problem:

- A matter or situation regarded as unwelcome or harmful and needing to be dealt with and overcome

According to its definition, a problem is something that requires action, and when talking about dealing and overcoming, we can say that it has to do with finding a solution, or a way out.

With this definition we are taking out of the table all those circumstances that are unwelcome or harmful but don't require any action. If there's nothing to do, then it's not a problem. It's a matter of acceptance. I'm not saying it's easy, I've been in a situation where my mind was not understanding that there was nothing to do, I would battle the reality not understanding, or not wanting to understand that it was life happening right there. So, identifying these situations will help us to start our healing process sooner.

Then, if there's something to do, it means that there's a solution, so it's not a problem either. In conclusion, the key is to find out what to do, but other than that, a problem is just a situation that we don't like and we were not expecting, so analyzing it, and finding a way of moving forward from your mind first, it's what will make a difference. Most of the times we are so involved in our feelings, the context, limiting ideas or beliefs and excuses, that we can't find a clear path.

So here is something that you can do in those moments:

Face the problem and ask yourself "What CAN I do?" then you will answer everything that you can't do. Ask yourself again but changing the intonation "WHAT can I do?" and here come the excuses. Again, "WHAT CAN I DO?" Eventually, after the fourth or fifth time, you will start to surrender, and then the options will start to come to your mind. There is always something that we can do, even if it is to set a limit on the waiting time.

Let's say that I am frustrated because my partner lives in another country and even though he has the opportunity to move to the US with me, he is not doing it, but he is saying that he will. After some time of waiting, there's nothing that I can do about it, I can't make him come to the US if he doesn't want to. But I am also frustrated because he is not here, and it's been two years since I moved, and this was supposed to be "our" project. So, I ask myself "What can I do?" I CAN set a limit on the time, I can let him know that I will wait for another six months, but after that, I can't keep on waiting. That information will give me sadness, but also relief. Because when I look at my future, at least I know that a year from now I won't be sad and frustrated because he is still not moving with me.

I hope this example was useful. In conclusion, we need to ask ourselves the same question consistently until we find a solution, because dead-end streets won't take us to the next level. We can also write it down to have better awareness of the answers.

To make sure that we stick to our decision, to our open-ended street, and we keep moving forward, we need to ask ourselves: "What structure-time, plans, and other factors do you need to create to make sure your endings happen?" Dr. Henry Cloud asked in Necessary Endings.

Some people use their friends, a family member, new activities that would keep them entertained and meeting new people. An accountability partner.

For me it was JOURNALING. I can't stress enough how useful, game changer and simple tool it is.

When I separated I started to use my journal. I did it because I've been through my mother's grief, and I've navigated it in a conscious manner, and I was feeling that it would be good not to forget some details. Especially because with time we only remember the great moments. And that is amazing, unless you're navigating through a breakup. So I started writing to make sure I didn't forget the sad parts, the difficulties, the relief I felt when I moved out.

To my surprise, I found a thought tracker. I don't know if that's a thing, but it is now for me!

I started to notice how my thoughts were evolving one day to the next. And through writing it down, I could appreciate the whole process.

I didn't have the need to read it back to remember the sadness I've been through. It was clear that we didn't work together as a couple. What I came back to read were my own evolving processes and changes in my thoughts.

I read it to refresh some moments for the book. I found that I wrote down my intentions on March 13. One of them was to meet new people. On March 14th I met my friend Cathy in the park. I didn't remember that sequence, but when I found it I couldn't believe it!

There's another time I asked for a sign. I was missing my mother a lot, I was not feeling well, and I wasn't finding her. The following day I found many signs, I remember that I read back the previous page to make sure that I was not crazy!

By now you may think I am, but trust me, if you start doing journaling you won't regret it!

Just for the record, I also write down my accomplishments, I keep track of my mood so I know I am making progress. I don't write down every day, I just write when I feel I have something. Sometimes I push myself a little bit, and I give myself ten minutes to write whatever has been in my mind that day. And works!

And this leads us to Pomodoro. Yes, "I gave myself ten minutes."

Pomodoro is a time management technique that helps us to be more efficient. It consists of working on twenty-five-minutes intervals and then taking short breaks.

I normally suggest doing intervals according to your workflow and your capacity for staying focused.

If you normally get distracted, then start with fifteen-minute intervals until you move to longer intervals. If short amounts of time won't be enough to execute a complete task, then use longer intervals.

To write this book I started with one-hour intervals, and then I started moving according to how I was feeling it. Sometimes I would sit down and write something in twenty minutes and then come back later. There were other moments when I could be sitting for a little longer than an hour. I normally push myself to get a little more done, it is important to have a limit, to know the limit, because the problem is that if I push myself too hard today, and I am not able to do anything tomorrow, then, there's no point on having done the effort, I am even becoming less efficient since I lost the whole day. So keeping track of the periods of time and being aware of how hard we are pushing ourselves, will make a huge difference regarding the efficiency of our performance.

Here are some questions to reflect on our goals:

- What does your best-self look like?
- How do you see yourself having a successful life?
- What is the next step you need to take to get closer to that vision?
- What is the next step you CAN take to get closer to your best self?
- When are you going to do it?
- How are you going to measure your progress?
- Is this plan realistic?

*Replace "your best self" for any other wish or objective you have and follow the questions.

JOURNAL IT

11

PLAN THE WORK...

IN THE PREVIOUS chapter we worked on setting a goal properly. In this chapter we will work on making a plan to achieve it.

As we already know, making a proper plan is one of the most important tasks to help us reach the objective, while making a bad plan is one of the main reasons that prevent people from achieving.

For me there at least two ways of making an accurate plan:

- From A to Z
- From Z to A

Going from A to Z:

I will consider A as today, and Z as the goal, and the ideal situation.

For us to get there we can start planning which are the next steps that we need to take, make a list in the order that they should happen and that way we will get through each letter.

I normally do it by breaking up tasks in the smallest way possible and organizing them by week or month.

The plan can be from A to Z, or we can set milestones that you will need to achieve, and use those milestones as smaller goals. So the plan would look like this:

A =>b =>c=> D

Being D a milestone.

After getting to D you can start planning the next steps.

This is a good option for long term goals, because we will plan for a shorter amount of time, let's say three months, and that will prevent us from being overwhelmed and anxious.

Preparing the whole plan at once may look overwhelming, as I said, so make sure that you are checking in with yourself and keeping your expectations realistic.

Considering those milestones is about taking into account those activities in the plan that may take flexible time, and when those activities become the neck of the bottle, we want to make sure that we specially consider them, so my suggestion would be to schedule around those tasks that could cause a delay.

The other way of doing it, Z to A, is similar, but it's reversed. We start from the ideal situation, or the end of the project, and we break it down until we get to our reality.

Some projects may look obvious to build from scratch, while there are others that are easier to be deconstructed.

Either way is fine.

In the second option, we are also working with milestones, and paying attention to the items that could get the project stuck.

For example, I am working with a coachee that is developing a commercial project on a piece of land. As he was making the plan, he found out that the place doesn't have water, and the installation, with the permits, may take a year. Despite the fact that he was planning from A to Z at the beginning, eventually, he had to make the master plan of the development and identify all those installations and permits that could potentially hold him back. He made those his focal points to get started, and postpone other investments until the place is ready to be constructed.

What I am trying to say is that we can plan how it suits us best, however our brain identifies the process. Regardless of the method, it is a must to identify the key tasks and how we will work around them.

Once we have the list of the activities we will need to do, we start planning the time frame.

First, we check our availability, we find the slots and we block them to work on our project. I'd rather be conservative than overscheduled.

So here's the deal, if we plan properly and realistically, we become achievers, we track processes and stay motivated. If we overschedule ourselves, we will be frustrated for not accomplishing the objectives and we will have to work on readjusting the plan, over and over again, this will cause more delays and we will lose motivation.

With that being said, we will assign those slots to the project, and then, we will show up as if it was another regular activity, because it is.

One of the top excuses is "I don't have time," and yes, I say it is an excuse because it seems almost impossible (I'm not saying it can't happen) that having twenty-four hours a day, you still don't have time. Let's say it in another way, "I need to find the time."

When we are looking for some time in our weekly schedule, we will start by setting our priorities. Every schedule looks different and all the priorities are valid. Once we have the priorities and the extra activities we will do if we have extra time, we go over the schedule.

If you still haven't found the time, don't worry, you can

use a timesheet, it consists of writing down every activity you do during the day. If you have a different schedule every day, you should do it for a week, but if your days look similar, then doing it for a couple of days will be enough. When I say that you should write down everything you do, I mean it, everything!

I promise that once you have your timesheet and you take some time to review it, you will find the opportunities of having that extra time that you are looking for.

Once you have your schedule ready, it is important to double check how realistic it is. If it seems realistic, then what I would do next is assign activities to those slots that I have available for my project. You can also show up and decide which task you will perform according to your mood, in this case, you still need to track time, so I suggest working with a thirty-, sixty-, ninety- day plan.

Of course, if it doesn't look realistic, make the adjustments needed.

Now you have some tools on how to make a plan. I'd like to add a couple of comments about time management. The way I see it, it is a habit that requires a skill.

Let me explain, having a balanced schedule is an ongoing process. It has to do with lots of daily decisions. In my experience, I used to be late all the time, I couldn't figure out the problem, until I started to pay more attention. Then, I used a timesheet, and I noticed that I wasn't taking into account the time that it takes to grab my stuff and get in the car. Let's say that I had to be somewhere at 6 o'clock p.m., I had a fifteen-minute drive, I would leave my chair at 5:45 p.m." By the time I got into the car, I was already arriving late. It may look silly, but I couldn't realize what was going on. The other problem I had was that I used to overschedule myself, I would make a list of five tasks I would like to perform during an afternoon, even though I knew it was impossible, but I was doing that to choose the activity. The problem is that I would end up being frustrated, because whatever I was accomplishing was never enough, and it was my fault, but I wasn't realizing that it was also extremely self-demanding, because I always had something to do, and I wasn't considering "resting" as an activity. So I was frustrated, tired, moody, not checking in with myself, always running from one place to the other one, never being fully present.

Once I detected all these bad habits I was having around my time management, I started to pay more attention. I also learned that being rested is part of being productive, so I started to spare time to relax and rest.

Nowadays, I ask myself about my energy and I choose an achievable amount of activities to do in a couple of hours. For instance, if it's Sunday, I am feeling lazy, so I think to myself "Which are the three most impactful activities that I need to do today that would make me have a better week?" And then, "what are you doing to celebrate the accomplishment?"

And I answer, let's say that the activities are cleaning the floor, organizing the clean clothes, and changing sheets. I normally give myself some time, let's say an hour, and when I am done, I'm having an ice cream, or taking a bath.

I've done it over and over again, and I even started to ask myself on Fridays "What activities would be impactful for me to have a better week?" so I perform them during the weekend.

And that's how I changed my habit, and now I choose intentionally which tasks I will perform, and when I will get them done, as a consequence, I have time to rest, I sleep better, and I feel more accomplished and calm. I stopped blaming traffic or using any other excuse, because I am normally not late any more, and I am even enjoying the drives. My stomach doesn't hurt anymore, because I am not in a constant rush, stressed and overwhelmed. I schedule with intention, awareness, and impact.

To develop a healthy time management habit, my suggestion is to start by defining how a balanced life looks like for you. Then, as I said before, define priorities. Ask and accept all the help that you have available, and think about how you could make your life easier.

What I mean about receiving help, I am talking about any friend or family member that can commit to executing any task from your checklist that would make your life easier. I am also talking about hiring someone even for a couple of hours a week, it can be four hours a week, and that would make a difference already, as well as the opportunity to build a team, even if it is small.

I shared my tip on how to delegate in the previous chapter.

Before accepting or organizing a big project, ask yourself if it is worthy to invest your time on it.

Yes, I said "invest." Time is a resource, and we only have twenty-four hours a day. The difference between investing and spending has to do with what we get back. When we invest, we are getting something out of it. Let's say that your project is to bake a cake with your daughter. Well, you are not only getting the cake, but what you are earning is the moment with her, the anecdote, the experience. When you spend your time baking a cake by yourself while your family is sleeping, you are getting the same cake that you could have bought, and you are just getting tired, so you are wasting or spending your time. You would be investing your time if you were doing something more impactful.

Again, this is just an example, I am trying to illustrate the importance of the experiences and that our time is valuable and priceless. We tend to lose sight of that, and we miss the important things that are all those moments that money can't buy. We spend so much time working, and that's fine, I understand that we need to pay bills, that's why working smart as well as being able to balance our schedule will make a difference in the way we live our lives.

With all these being said, I also recommend setting our daily goals or activities ahead of time. It can be the previous day, or even in the morning, but being organized will help us to be in control of what we can control. There are always some unpredictable events, and we deal with them as they arise. In the meantime, we will try to stick to our plan.

To sum up:

For the plan:

- Define A and Z
- Identify milestones and bottle necks
- Breakdown as much as you can all the tasks
- Schedule a time to work in your project
- Show up
- Use the matrices from chapter 10
- If you have the chance, build a team, and delegate

For time management:

- Ask yourself "How does life balance look like for me?"
- Use a timesheet to track your activities and identify opportunities
- Make a list of priorities and extra activities
- Assign your project to your schedule as any other activity
- Set a time frame for your project (Let's say that it will last 6 months)
- Set deadlines

- Work with a specific activity plan or a 30/60/90-day plan
- Prioritize impactful activities
- Make conscious choices: What to do? What is the best day and time to do that?
- Reflect everyday: What do you want to accomplish today? How much time will I give myself to complete that task? How am I going to celebrate it?
- Accept all the help available

Now, you only need to find the best way for you to hold yourself accountable, and which is the best method to keep track of all these new strategies and take massive action. There is no need for you to start to implement everything at the same time, just pick a couple of small actions that require a little energy and that are important and impactful. You can try a journal; you can try any other tech tool that you feel like, and just make it happen!

JOURNAL IT

12

... AND WORK THE PLAN!

*PURPOSE STATEMENT: At the end of this chapter my reader will iden-
tify the potential setbacks and how to tackle them*

In this chapter I will help you identify and tackle those
circumstances and limiting beliefs that normally prevent us
from executing the plan.

Procrastination: whoever is not guilty of procrastinating
can throw the first stone.

It is the action of postponing or delaying something.
We've all done it at some point because we don't know where
to start, how to do it, maybe it's not our favorite task, and
many other reasons.

The truth is that the sooner we take care of it, the better.
To avoid procrastination, I assign those tasks that I don't like
doing to a specific day, and when that day comes, I just move
through them. Some people say, "eat the ugly frog in the
morning," that is good also if you have daily tasks you tend
to procrastinate.

I always encourage my coachees to find a radical solution, this means that you won't have to deal or worry about

this task ever again. The best solution normally is delegating the tasks that we don't want to do. If we can't delegate them, then we need to identify them, and make sure we rip the band aid fast so it doesn't hurt, that means that my suggestion is to set up a day and time and stick to the schedule and complete the task fast and efficient, and then give ourselves a good time by doing something that we enjoy.

For example, I had this coachee that owns a party supplies store. He didn't like to manage social media, and procrastination was preventing him from getting customers to sign up for the classes they were dictating. So, he would pay a teacher to go and lead a class, and she would charge him the same for two pupils or for eight. It was a direct loss for his business, it was loss of income even if it wasn't negative profit.

The solution was that he offered the teacher to manage social media, and they would share the income in a different way. This was better, because even though now he was paying her more money, he wasn't making that much for his lack of execution. Also, he stopped having that task that on top of not wanting to do it, he was feeling guilty by acknowledging that he was losing money, or at least, not making as much as he could.

It was a win-win solution, the teacher was earning more money, having the opportunity to manage social media, which was giving her more exposure, and for him, he just deleted the task from his to-do list.

This was a radical sustainable solution. So, every time that you're trying to implement a new system, it doesn't matter if it's to avoid procrastination, or if it's just to delegate, ask yourself:

- Is it radical? This means that you won't have to worry about this again.

- Is it sustainable? This means that you can keep the system over time.

Another huge hold back that is not always recognized as so is multitasking. Yes, multitasking is a huge myth!

There is not such a thing as doing more than one task that requires our focus at the same time. We can listen to music while we work, but we can't have a conversation while reading, you are doing one or the other, or neither.

To switch tasks or moving from one task to another one and then back again to the first one may have worked twenty years ago when we didn't have smartphones, we had only one or two email accounts, and information was not moving so fast. We were not as stimulated and distracted by devices or social media.

The truth is that multitasking prevents us from being efficient and completing tasks properly. Also, it makes our brain more tired, causing more stress because of the effort that we do by trying to stay focused on each task, and therefore, this process damages our brain.

Studies show that multitasking decreases productivity and efficiency by at least 40 percent.

With this information now you will be able to make better choices on your working style. Another problem with multitasking is that it prevents us from identifying clear priorities, this means that when everything is a priority, nothing is important.

To get more focused and intentional, you can go back to chapter 10 and check the matrices that will help you to choose by importance and impact.

When it comes to concentration, what you need to know is that it can be developed. I like practicing with the Pomodoro technique. It consists of working twenty-five minutes straight and taking a five-minute break. After four or five rounds you take a longer break, like fifteen or twenty minutes.

The way I apply it is slightly different, I encourage my coachees to set a timer for time they have available, or they feel comfortable with, even if it is fifteen minutes or one hour. Then, you work on your to-do straight for that amount of time, and ten out of ten times people get surprised about how much they can accomplish in a fraction of time when they are only focused on working with time, versus working against time.

There is another way, let's say that I need to finish a task, so I will get ready to perform it and commit not to leave the spot or get distracted until I am done with it, I would also give myself some time to complete it. And then, after accomplishing it I would give myself a nice break or a price.

Nobody wants to be sitting for a couple of hours to complete a task that could be done in thirty minutes.

By trying this you will start to notice how much you can accomplish and how many activities you can include in twenty-four hours. This has to do with time management, and what we reviewed in the last chapter, where I mentioned that this is a game changer. To be conscious and intentional with the way we use our time, it's a habit. Remember, time is a resource, as we use it, we need to make it count!

Training your brain, training yourself to be fully connected and aware, being impactful, or not, the most important thing is that you have resources available and how you choose to live your life is up to you, as long as you understand that you are making the choice.

Part of developing your concentration is to control the distractions. The number one distraction is the cellphone, and then emails. Other than that, we can identify internal and external distractions. Internals are those that depend on us, and external are those that come from the environment.

It is important to identify them and neutralize them. If distractions are internal, then, you need to set yourself up for success through leaving those distractions aside. For instance, not checking your phone, forwarding calls, and avoiding checking your emails. If you review Pomodoro technique, I encourage people to choose the time of the slots because I want to make sure that everyone feels comfortable. If you consider that you can't go longer than fifteen minutes without checking your phone, then work on fifteen-minute blocks, and that's fine, take a five-minute break, no longer than that, and keep on moving forward with your task.

As per external distractions we have those that we can't fully control, but most of them can be managed. If there's a noise that is not letting you work, or someone speaks to you, or even if it's crowded or cluttered, most of the time you have the opportunity to choose where to work, to wear headphones so people around you know that you are busy or unavailable. Also consider working in a coffee shop or any place that helps you find your focus.

If you are working from home and you have kids, as some of my coachees, you may need to strategize around their times. You can make the most with the time you have available when they take naps. You can always look for and use some help, let's say that someone can watch your kids for a couple of hours a couple of times a week. Even for small periods, if you learn to be focused, you will increase your efficiency a lot.

One of my coachees during this process found out that if she dedicated between twenty and thirty minutes to her kids, making sure that they have everything that they normally ask for, she can work straight for an hour, or maybe a little more, so it is about finding your own way, there's not an only solution that works for everyone.

Motivation tends to be a hold back also. I've heard many

people expecting to have their motivation back. Sometimes we are stuck without even knowing it. Being stuck feels like lack of willingness, complaining about everything, being short of time, being frustrated, spending more time taking care of the urgent matters than the important, feeling that you are ready to get to next level and you don't know how to get there, and feeling that you are not taking advantage of your full potential.

If you are there, my suggestion is to take action, don't wait until you are desperate, start today!

If you've been there, I'm happy that you got unstuck and that you're moving forward.

As always, there are many ways of getting to the same result, so I will try to help by mentioning the most common ways.

Anna came to see me when she was feeling just like that. In the first conversation we had, we talked about her personal and professional life. She was concerned about the example she was setting for her kids. So we started with little steps to move forward.

The first, and from my point of view, most important shift is perspective. She started taking a glass of water every morning, that way she would be proving herself that she was committed and consistent. She also started to practice gratitude, not only writing it down but also vocalizing it. This means that she was specially focused on being more grateful and loving to her family and friends. In addition, she challenged herself to try to stop complaining about everything.

If we go over the actions, there are two specific, and then two other activities that would help her be more aware. It may sound like a lot, but it is pretty straightforward.

Two weeks after her first session she was already another person. Let me tell you, she made the commitment of working on those things at the same time, then, she kept on adding little actions for her daily schedule. Over some time, she noticed that some of them were more impactful than others, so she kept the practices that were more useful for her.

These little things help her with the change in her filters. We all know that 10 percent is what happened, and 90 percent is how we react. The filters are the perceptions that we have of reality. If we are stuck and in a constant negative mood, we will always react in a negative way. However, if we are positive and receive what may come in peace, we will get through it in a better way. We will be open to learn and capitalize the situation.

As Anna did, she has a difficult boss. We worked on empathizing, changing the perspective, looking for the opportunities that working with this woman may bring, then, we worked on how to react towards her and get to the results in a way that was easier for her. Over a couple of sessions, she is not only having a better relationship with her boss, but also, her boss chose her to represent the area in many important events, which is a good opportunity for Anna.

So, if you feel stuck and you are ready to take action, you can start by showing some commitment and consistency, practicing gratitude, and asking yourself "What can I do?." It's tricky because when I ask people "What can you do about this?" a few times they say "nothing" and then a lot of times they start telling me everything that they "can't" do. Here my suggestion is to grab a pen and paper and start writing down what you can actually do, and you will notice that making a list of the things that you can't do won't make any difference and won't take you anywhere. Then, try again writing what you can do!

Last, but not least, when you catch yourself criticizing or

complaining, stop right there and make yourself think about the same situation with love and gratitude. Get out of your head, don't make a positive perspective and then "but" and keep on stuck in your comfort zone by doing nothing. All that negativity, all that complaining are just excuses, and we don't like them, at least I don't!

If you are reading this chapter before chapter 4, then I encourage you to go to the "Gifts" section and review this topic.

And this is how we get into talking about "The comfort zone." I read something that said that "Our comfort zone is the room decorated with our favorite excuses," and I couldn't agree more!

Through my path to get where I am today, I made some hard and uncomfortable decisions. I left my country, my family, my friends, a steady job position, and came to Miami because I was looking for a different opportunity and challenge.

A couple of years after that, I came to the agreement with my sister that I would stop managing the business that we co-managed at that time. Yes, that decision was triggered by my mother's diagnosis, but I'm sharing this so you don't wait for that trigger. After that, I sold my half of the business to my sister and started my own coaching practice.

Up until this point, all those decisions had more to do with my professional than my personal life.

Until this year when Andrew told me that he thought that we needed to separate, that he was trying to picture his future and he was not sure if I was in that picture anymore, that he loved me, but in a different way. That our relationship needed work and he was not going to do it. That we could keep on having the same relationship, but that relationship was all he could offer, so if I chose to stay, it would be accepting that for me that marriage was not working.

It took me two months to figure out how to move forward. I had to leave his home, obviously, but there were moments that it was not clear if we were making progress or not. As I said, after two months of processing I left. There were a couple of reflections that helped me take action for good:

How do I want to be a year from now? Do I still want to be frustrated and miserable as I am today?

What fact is there other than my hope that something will change tomorrow?

And then, "fear" got in the chat, so I started thinking about how I would be in a year? Would I eventually meet someone else? Can I afford to live by myself? And a lot of other questions.

It all came down to the acknowledgement that I'd rather live with the uncertainty of what the future was holding for me than with the certainty of being not loved and unhappy. And clarity hit me, the uncertainty of the future, was the certainty of happiness.

No matter what, I am committed to my happiness, so even if I have to make hard or uncomfortable decisions, I know that I will be fine. Indeed I am!!

The last question here is:

How committed are you to your happiness?

And from my perspective, this question has no grays, it's either black or white, you are committed to your happiness, or you are committed to your unhappiness.

Among those choices I made, many times I heard the word "failure," and it has to do with the fact that things were ending.

I learned a lot about endings when I read "Necessary Endings" from Dr. Henry Cloud. I strongly recommend that book, it was a complete game changer for me.

As we come to an ending in this chapter, my expectation

is for you to move to the next one with the certainty that there's always something to do, there's always a way out, the question is "What are you willing to give up to get where you want to go?."

JOURNAL IT

VI

PURPOSE

13

SHINE BRIGHT!

THE WAY I see the purpose is like a light. It's alive, it's the energy, it's what lets us see the path, make us take charge and choose our next step. It's a self-organizing life aim that simulates goals, promotes healthy behaviors, and gives meaning to life. When your authentic purpose becomes clear, you will be able to share it with the world!

The importance of finding the purpose is that it is proven that people with a purpose live longer and have a better quality of life. In addition, through our purpose we can help others to find theirs.

In the case of working with a team, this discovery will contribute to better performance at work, since there are studies that show that people with a purpose are more productive.

Purpose: the reason for which something is done or created or for which something exists.

If we analyze the definition, we realize that it makes sense that it is so important, it is the reason why something exists. To exist by definition is "To have objective reality or being." Then, to have a purpose is what keeps our light on, living, existing. The closer we get to it, and the more intense and impactful it is, the brighter we shine.

Here are some questions to start thinking about it:

- Have you ever thought about your purpose?
- How do you relate to your purpose today?
- What does purpose mean for you?
- What is your purpose today?

Statistics show that people that work with a purpose and a passion are in the 84th percentile of productivity. While people without a purpose are closer to the 20th percentile.

Then, having a purpose and a passion will help you to move forward faster and easier in your career, and of course, in your life.

We may not be used to thinking that long term, or to observe the whole picture when we are looking for a job, but paying attention to details, and again, being intentional is what will make a difference in our life in the long term.

When I think about the purpose, as I said, I automatically relate it with light, I see the purpose as the impact that we want to create, as the reason why we want to be remembered, as the way that we will transcend this life and this body. The stories that will be told about us, our legacy. So even after we are gone from Earth, the light will keep on shining and illuminating others.

When I was asked to deliver a talk about purpose, I did some research, and along the way I used my mother as an example, because she lived her life on purpose, she had one, and she was extremely happy, regardless of having battled cancer for thirteen years. She could always see the good in things, she was grateful, she was sweet, passionate, she honored her values, she used her gifts for the greater good.

When she passed away, one of my biggest fears was that

she may be forgotten. A year and a half after those moments, I am sure that she will always be remembered, for her legacy, for her joy, her laugh, for the great willingness she's always had, for her strength, for her huge heart. And anybody that knows her can say the same, not only her children. She still shines bright!

My mother was also a strong woman, she raised five kids, with my father, but she was at home with us most of the time, you don't play with a mother of five, especially if the first four kids are two years or less apart.

I remember her saying "Do it well on purpose! If you have good habits, you will be virtuous, if you have bad habits, you will be vicious."

It wasn't until recently that this expression gained another weight, the "Do it well on purpose," it is such a strong statement, despite the fact that it's simple and it doesn't sound that strong. Now I know that all the time, she was teaching us to make purposeful choices.

For me, my purpose has always been to have a foster home for kids, or a charity foundation. That was my biggest dream, to be able to help kids. I always felt that somehow, I owed it to life, because of how lucky I've been to be born exactly where I was born.

Years passed by, and my desire to help others didn't change, but the shape of the project did.

Through leadership coaching I became a strong believer that we are all leaders at some point. It doesn't matter if until now you didn't notice it, just take a moment, and think about the people around you, who are watching you, who are you creating an impact on, even if it is not in the exact moment, the consequences of our decisions, and the consistency or inconsistency of them, are noticeable. So, it is important for us to consider our behaviors and the impact they will have on everyone. This means that at every moment we have the opportunity to inspire someone, or to hurt or let down someone else. It is a choice, and it requires commitment and awareness. As every good habit, it becomes a virtue circle. Being a leader is a responsibility, we shape others. You may be leading your household, your friends, a football team, or you may be a CEO leading a company, being a leader has the same principles for everyone.

To be a leader, first you need to acknowledge it, and also, you need to have followers. Well, the most important follower is yourself, because as a leader, your masterpiece is your life. When I came to this thought I decided that even if the only thing I am leading is my life, I will do it in the best way I can. So I started thinking about how I had envisioned myself, and what would create an impact to find myself living that life in the immediate future.

To help me with that future picture of myself, I created a vision board including all the areas of my life that were important to me and that would determine the priorities. I spent some time thinking about, creating intentions on the pictures I was choosing, selecting phrases and expressions that would make sense. And I started moving toward it. I keep the vision board close to me in my office, so I keep my motivation and objectives clear.

Being a leader is a lifestyle, this means that there are several qualities that define and represent you, if you are a good leader, you have good habits, then you are a virtuous leader. When you are a bad leader, you have bad habits, you are a vicious person. There are many grays in between, and it all depends on the perspectives that we analyzed in previous chapters. For me the complicated leaders are those that don't recognize themselves as so, and for that reason, they don't lead their lives. They don't make conscious, impactful, and intentional decisions. They just go through life with the flow, in a passive way, complaining about life events.

There is another group that don't recognize themselves as leaders, and they lead their lives going with the flow, they accept what life gives them with love and gratitude and go actively manifesting themselves. I love this group. It always seemed to me like they learned how to live in advance.

When I came to this understanding, the way I wanted to create an impact changed. I coach leaders, because leaders create leaders. Also, because I learned that when we are born we don't know about certain matters, such as bullying, discrimination, racism, feminism, among others. So if I am committed to helping kids, I should start by talking with the people that are teaching and shaping those kids minds.

There was another turning point in my purpose. It was the day my grandmother passed away. That day I realized that I was the eldest female in my family, yes, I have two amazing and powerful sisters, and I trust that the three of us can make it through anything, but that doesn't mean that I was 32, they are slightly younger than me, and that neither of us had the experience that we may need to go through a lot of events that life will present, happy events such as having kids, I am not talking about sad or unfortunate events.

I discussed it with them, and we came to the conclusion that we have a female net that will be there for us no matter what, cousins of my parents, friends of my mother.

I said that it was a turning point because I couldn't stop thinking about how fortunate we are. First of all because we are grown up people, we lack some experience, but we are capable of making decisions and coming up with solutions, we are educated and resourceful women. Then, I started to think about all the kids that are in the same situation and they need a net, someone that can help them to make the best decision, or even a good one. So I decided that when the time comes, I will create a mentoring program, I will call it "net-familying," for all those kids and young people that need assistance to move forward without having the experience, the education, or resources.

I got enthusiastic with the project and left the line of the leadership, excuse me.

So going back, when relating leadership to purpose, we need to make sure that our style is aligned with our mission. We can go over leadership styles, however, I consider that it doesn't have to do with the core of this book, and also, what I am talking about, is the way you feel comfortable leading. From my perspective there are as many leadership styles as leaders, so in this book we will stick to the idea of finding a way to lead that makes us feel comfortable and gives us joy.

Even though I encourage you to think about this topic and choose your main qualities and values, I will share with you the two qualities that I consider key to be a great leader: empathy and compassion.

Let's check these words:

Empathy:

- the ability to understand and share the feelings of another.

Compassion:

- a feeling of deep sympathy and sorrow for another who is stricken by misfortune, accompanied by a strong desire to alleviate the suffering.

Empathy is understanding the feeling of the other person as well as the ability to put ourselves in their position. To do this, we have to know: what that feeling is and what is the cause and the context of it. This way, we'll understand it.

Compassion is relieving others' pain, it's sympathy. Although we understand the feeling, we don't always know what the context is, or the cause. Compassion is simply about giving that relief. Some examples of compassion are helping someone in need, giving a hug to someone who's crying, social assistance in the face of natural disasters, among others.

These days with everything that's going on, I truly believe that we must exercise both empathy and compassion. Exercising compassion means treating people in a more lovely way. This way we can relieve pain, most of the time without even knowing we are doing it. And remember, even when we can't understand something with our mind, we should be able to comprehend from our heart.

Being a leader requires being able to make hard decisions as well, focused on the greater good. As Dr. Henry Cloud said in "Necessary Endings," There's a difference between hurting and harming.

In the early stages of my career, I remember that it was hard for me to make some decisions, for instance to terminate a team member. Until I came to the understanding that my responsibility as the head of the organization was to keep the business running steady and smoothly. This means that I couldn't let bad apples stay in the organization. My job was to watch for the greater good and prioritize the well-being of the best team members.

The same happens when we are not ready or willing to have difficult conversations, set boundaries, or discipline our team members, because they may understand that everything is fine and that the company doesn't need them that much, or that they are not as important as they are, so they don't see any difference if they show up in the morning or not. To be able to address these issues, even when it means that someone is not reaching the standards and needs to leave the company, it all leads to a better functioning and a healthy business.

As I said, for many years I struggled to make those decisions until I understood my real job: keep the business running. I had to do it for the team members and for the business itself.

Being a business owner, an entrepreneur, or any kind of leader, is about making hard decisions, and to make them in the best possible way so we don't hurt anyone in the process.

Going one more time back to our purpose, leading by example considering everything we went over before, means to lead by your purpose, to illuminate not only your path, but also, helping others to follow theirs. Yes! Your purpose is that important! So, if you find yourself missing leading opportunities, this is your call to start taking those opportunities and make a difference. How would you like to create an impact? How would you like to be remembered? How would you like to keep on shining forever?

Here are some extra questions:

- What is the reason you get up every morning? What does fulfill you?
- What would you like to be remembered for? What message would you like to send? What would you like to be proud of yourself for?
- Who must you fearlessly become?
- How will the world be better off thanks to you having been on this earth?
- What is the next step you can take to get closer to your purpose?
- How does your job/company align to your purpose?

Take a moment to check if there's any opportunity to end or change something:

- How do you see yourself in a year?
- Would you like to be dealing with the same issues a year from now?
- Would you like to be bothered and frustrated about the same task/person/behavior a year from now?
- Is there any fact that indicates that something will be different tomorrow?
- What needs to change?
- How realistic is that change?
- What can you do on a daily/weekly/monthly basis to get closer to your vision?

JOURNAL IT

14

DO IT ON PURPOSE!

To LIVE through your purpose has to do with owning your truth.

Along the book I've been sharing personal stories and some of my coachees experiences to illustrate the importance of making choices that are aligned with your own truth.

Your truth has to do with your opinion.

Many times, I've witnessed people sharing thoughts and other people expressing their opinion.

Let's take a moment to review some definitions:

Opinion:

- a view or judgment formed about something, not necessarily based on fact or knowledge

Feedback:

- information about reactions to a product, a person's performance of a task, etc. which is used as a basis for improvement.

Truth/true:

- in accordance with fact or reality
- accurate or exact

As we can appreciate in these definitions, when we talk about opinion, we are talking about the point of view that a person has about certain topics, without any foundation such as knowledge or experience. However, when we talk about feedback, we are talking about information, by introducing "truth," we are talking about facts, and most importantly, it is used for improvement. It's also fair to say that the truth depends on the narrator, if we are not talking about accurate or exact facts, and we are talking about reality, it may be different for different people.

It is a good distinction to make, so I strongly recommend starting paying attention to what other people are telling us, and consider it accordingly.

Nowadays there are many "controversial" decisions that each of us make according to our own truth.

I've always considered becoming a single mother if by the time I was ready to have a child I didn't have a partner. It doesn't mean that I wouldn't prefer to have a partner, what it means is that love may come later than my desire to have a kid.

If I was to become a single parent, I decided that I would adopt. The reason is that for me, going through a pregnancy and a birth without a partner would mean that I would need other members of my family to commit to my project. Also, I would be making the decision that my child won't have a father figure. In my head I am subtracting from his/her life.

However, by adopting, I wouldn't have to involve other people on my project, I wouldn't face any risk or difficulty throughout the pregnancy or birth. And what is more, I would be an addition to that person's life, so instead of subtracting, I would already be a plus.

For me, people add or subtract, there are no neutrals. Again, it's my opinion, so based on this, I want to be a plus!

This is an extremely personal thought. It is not right, or wrong. It doesn't mean that I agree or disagree with other parent or family forms. It means that I am honoring my own truth. I have everything that seems important to me covered, considering my own experience, knowledge, and circumstances.

This doesn't mean that is the only way I am considering adoption, I would like to adopt in any circumstance, with or without a partner, but that is a decision I may have to share with another person, or not, it's a different circumstance and it's not on the table right now.

As well as the fact that I am considering freezing eggs, to keep my options open.

I don't discuss this with everyone. I may share my opinion, with certainty and conviction, I normally don't leave room for opinions in these matters, that's why I only share those thoughts with my closest circle.

Then, why am I sharing this with you?

Because a couple of days ago, I was having dinner with some friends. They are all married and in their early thirties. One of them told me that her sister, who is 29 years old and just broke up with her boyfriend, is considering freezing eggs, and she said "I told her that it's not necessary, that she still has time! That she doesn't have to worry" and that triggered me, so I told her "We all know that we have time, she just wants to keep her options open. Did you inform yourself about the process and the best time to do that procedure?" of course she said "no." Opinion, feedback, and truth.

When I was younger, just a couple of years ago, I used to be like her sister. I used to express my thoughts in a way that was almost inviting others to share their opinion. I changed, I stopped doing that, I learned that people do whatever they want without asking for my permission or my opinion, and I should only care about my own thoughts, because I am the one being in charge of my decisions and the consequences they may have. I am in charge of choosing how to live my life.

To own my truth helped me to express myself from confidence. My understanding is that some opinions are worth hearing, and those that are not adding any value to the discussion I would just pretend that didn't happen. I may sound arrogant, but it's not about that, it's about being aligned and in peace with myself. Having my mind, body and soul connected. It's about consistently making conscious choices that would lead me to the place I want to be.

Owning my truth set me free. It all came down to understanding that those unique qualities that made me be myself and were not up to the social standards, became my strength.

That being committed to myself, my toughness, my determination, made me be here today. What defines each of us is not what life throws at us, it's how we navigate it, how we stand up and keep on going.

I recall many times throughout my life when I thought to myself "I just want to do what I want to do, when I want to do it and How I want" and the ultimate situation was when I left my home with Andrew. I've been feeling worthless, walking on eggshells and I was ready to build my own life, with or without a partner. I decided I wouldn't let any mandate rule my decisions anymore. I decided I would question myself on those decisions, "Do I want to become a mother?" and after some time, I am discovering that even though I would like to be a mother at some point in my life, most of my passion and motivation today comes from challenges and my job, and that I still have many others to face. It all starts there, why should I hide it?

Somehow, I never thought I would be at thirty-three writing a book, being a coach, living in another country, but all those things happened as a result of the decisions I made. None of them were in vain. I have no regrets; I learned and capitalized every experience. Yes, many times I asked myself "What am I doing here?" when I moved to Miami. It's been a while since the last time that that question crossed my mind, I guess it has to do with my wake-up call, with the fact that I decided to be in charge, with all the work I've been doing to get to know myself better, to set boundaries, to stop living according to others' expectations or social mandates. I'm tired of hearing women talking about their age and that we must hurry to have kids, I am done with that, there are options, it's never too late. Let's do whatever we want and avoid anxiety, sadness and "what ifs?." Let's speak up about our choices respecting them. And do it on purpose, because you never know who is hearing, observing, or being inspired and supported by your bravely.

I am proud and grateful for every person that is living according to their own truth, that is following its purpose, because they make this world a better place, and they are an infinite source of inspiration. I wish I can inspire someone as many people have inspired me to follow my dreams, to find my purpose in life and to work toward it!

Since I am aligned with myself and my own truth, I am laughing more. I am laughing at myself. I don't even think about myself, it became unconscious to be connected and comfortable, therefore, I notice when I'm not.

Even some people noticed that it seems that I am enjoying life more.

Through some analysis, I came to the conclusion that it has to do with a limiting belief that I used to have. I grew up believing that for me to "deserve" to enjoy, I had to go through some hard work or sacrifice. Essentially, joy was "deserved."

For me, everything is wrong with that assumption. Joy and happiness are not deserved, we make them happen, they depend on us. It's not about how hard you worked to go on vacation, there are a lot of people that spend their whole life traveling and on vacation, and they chose how to make that happen, and in that choice there is no sacrifice. They just choose an activity or a job or a lifestyle that lets them live in that way.

The problem for me is that I used to arrive on vacations or any other plan that I was supposed to enjoy, late, stressed, with a migraine, because I would over work before the plan to "deserve" the joyful moment, but there was no joyful moment, because I was exhausted, and what is even worse, I would feel guilty for not enjoying it after all the sacrifice I've done to get there.

A couple of years ago I realized that those people that were living a more relaxed life, was because they chose to, they made the choices that lead them to have that lifestyle. They probably worked hard for some time, made difficult decisions, and kept on moving toward the goal they have set for themselves. In my experience it is doable. I chose to slow down, to respect my body and mind. I was so anxious and stressed managing the company, I was dealing with tasks that were triggering those sensations, so I chose to do something that would bring me joy. I still work hard, but I have a more flexible schedule that I manage. I am still in contact with people, I love that. I'm still trying to create an impact, and I am doing it from another place.

Here is how I understand "happiness as a choice" now:
First of all, I used to deeply dislike this expression.

Now I like it much, it seems I understood it, so I will share my understanding just in case you are just like me.

This phrase exempts those around from the responsibility of one's happiness. Although it is right, over time I understood that no one can make you happy, but I have found myself in situations where I chose to be happy, and someone caused me sadness, and there I understood: No one can make you happy, but someone can cause you joy or sadness. In another words, someone can make you laugh or cry, and when "being happy is a choice," it has to do with choosing to surround yourself with people who bring you joy (at least for most of the time). As I said before, people are a plus or a minus, choose pluses!

I feel like it assumes that we must be happy all the time, I have felt pressured to be happy. It is not like this! Happiness is like everything in life, one day it rains and one day the sun shines, and it has to rain for the sun to shine, and vice versa. All people go through moments of anguish, sadness, disappointment, frustrations, tiredness, and none of these emotions are happiness. However they are legit and natural, and if we accept them and accept ourselves in those moments, when the best feelings come we will have more intense moments of happiness. When "Being happy is a choice," it is because if we accept our emotions and we go through them with awareness, moments of happiness come, and we live them fully. On the contrary, if we force ourselves to "be happy," we are not giving room to the rest of the emotions, and then we do not process. This makes it more difficult for us to connect with ourselves and learn.

What about moments of absolute sadness that do not depend on you? For example, the death or illness of a loved one. How do we do in those seasons? "Being happy is a choice" means that we can choose to put forth effort to get ahead, choose to work to feel happy again when we are ready, and I promise, you will feel happiness and hope again. In the meantime, stay still until we are healed enough to start moving again.

What about sad moments related to certain life circumstances? For example, when something gets to an end or when we are in a place with an external factor that does not allow us to "choose that happiness." In this case, "being happy is a choice" means closing that cycle, ending, or changing whatever is necessary to get to the moment where we can be happy, nobody and nothing can stop us from making the choice of moving towards joy, fulfillment, and happiness.

Happiness is a concept. How each one understands it depends on the life experience that each person has had, there is no formula, nor a singular way to feel happy.

Being happy for me means looking for, finding, recognizing, accepting, loving, and asking ourselves "how do I feel? What do I want to do today and now?" And respecting our answer, because that will allow us to live fully, it is like carrying an umbrella when it rains, and sunglasses when it's sunny. It is about feeling each feeling and breaking through them!

When we talk about fulfillment, we talk about the things that fill our soul. That causes us happiness and satisfaction in the body.

When do you feel like this?

It happens to me when I practice coaching, and although I am a coach, it surprises me each time when I help people, when they make progress, and that fulfills me!

One of my coachees, Matt, was telling me that he was feeling comfortable at work. Over a couple of minutes he said that many times, so I asked him, "what does comfortable mean for you?" and he answered that it has to do with the perks, flexibility, salary, position, vacation time, among others.

A couple of minutes after that he said that he was uncomfortable at work. So again, I asked him what it was about. And he said that he was not feeling useful, passionate, or using his full potential. It was not fulfilling him.

He kept on talking and explaining why it was important for him to be part of that company and fight for his position, and every other moment he was going back to the same reflection, this job position was not fulfilling him, he was not motivated, he was frustrated and miserable. He was clearly stuck.

At some point in the coaching session, he realized that it would be good for him to assess other options, and while doing it I asked him "what was he willing to give up?" and then he said "everything! I'm just realizing that I can't keep on spending my life being miserable just because this is a family business and my father founded it."

So this was an awakening moment for him, it was the moment he realized that he better get in charge of his decisions and choose happiness.

If you feel the same way I hope you find the courage and guidance to get in the path of joy and fulfillment. I am here for you, and I know there's a path that would take you to that place you're looking for, most of the time, it all starts with a brave decision.

With this reflection, I am asking you:

- What is your comfort level in each area of your life?
- What does "being comfortable" look like for you?
- What are you missing to feel happy?
- How would that area of your life be if it was amazing?

- What are you willing to give up to reach that vision?
- What does it take for you to get to that vision?
- How can you get closer to your purpose?
- What opportunities are you missing to lead with purpose in your personal and professional life?

JOURNAL IT

VII

"BE A WARRIOR, NOT A WORRIER"

15

"EXCUSES" LEFT THE CHAT

INDECISION:

What happens when we have a hard time making decisions?

We are in eternal circles of thoughts in which we debate which is the best option. It happens to us in more important things, and it happens to us in nonsense, the problem is not only the delay in making decisions, but also the time and energy that we dedicate to a debate that fundamentally exists due to a doubt or insecurity.

I think that for these situations there are many solutions, I share my method: Policies

So I call them! I define policies, then when making a decision I take it according to the policy.

How do I define policies? According to certain information and parameters. I do a preliminary investigation, for example, if I have to choose a computer, I define the budget that I have to spend, I identify the most important indicators regarding the qualities of the article. I always try to deal with brands or places that I know, I don't go around a lot, I go to the place, informed and ready to make a decision. I find the models that fit the parameters I defined and make a decision.

As a policy:

- Define a budget
- Choose brands that already worked for me in the past, and avoid those that haven't
- Get informed about the most important characteristics the item should have
- Go to the store when I am ready to execute the decision
- Saving time and energy in this type of matter is saving money.

There are other examples, such as Mr. E, who, when I told him about my policy strategy, answered me: "I have a new policy, I just decided that I am going to sign up for all tennis tournaments."

Mr. E. has been playing tennis for a year. Every time he has a tournament, he spends a lot of time debating whether to sign up or not, because he loses, and he considers that he is not that good, which causes him frustration and annoyance. After spending that time, and based on that thought, he shows up to play without any additional preparation, and he definitely loses the tournament.

With this example we realize the importance of having an exercised decision making. Creating policies is not the only way, it is about each one creating their own method, the one that works for each of us, because the decision-making process is as important as the final decision, in some cases as we have seen is not only about the time and the energy we lose, but more importantly, it has to do with the attitude with which we face the activity, and consequently the result we obtain.

There are many other situations that are applicable to policies. For instance, when I went to New Orleans, I was doing a walking tour. Before going to the tour, I had a number in my head as a budget for tours. Then, when I arrived, I found out that we were only four people, so when I made the number of the money that the guide would make in that tour I started doubting about how much I would give her. I had cash ready, but when the time came, I asked "Do you accept Zelle?" instead of sticking to the number I had in mind, and instead of making a decision right there, I procrastinated, so I told her I would send her the money later. I've been with the decision in my head going back and forth the whole day. When I got back to my room, it was time to make the decision, so it was right there when I decided that as a policy, I would stick to my budget, no matter how many people were on the tour.

The following days I kept on going to different tours, and I found the same guide with a lot of people in her walks, so I felt better.

I am telling this story because even though it may look silly, it took so much time and energy that it was even ridiculous!

When we explored Mr. E's decision-making process, feeling frustrated, and negative thinking, the question I asked him was: Are you setting yourself up for success?

And he told me no, that he was clearly setting himself up for failure.

Reviewing the definitions of competition, winning, and losing, I would like us to re-signify it. In a coaching session with a Dr., I asked her "Are two people alike?" To which she replied, "Even homozygous twins are not the same," so based on this, I invite you to rethink the competition.

Let us rule out that competition in sports is the fundamental basis of tournaments, as well as in other aspects, but here we are talking about daily life, of people whose daily work does not include competition as part of their job.

Personally, I think that the competition, based on this information, does not exist as such, or at least it is absurd. Because the reality is that we are human beings and our performance depends on many factors. By modifying this concept, and understanding that we compete with ourselves to try to be our best version, which includes development and evolution, we begin to reconvert the meaning of winning and losing, of success and failure.

Having read this, what would be your definition of winning and losing?

Mine: I win when I give my 100 percent, regardless of whether that 100 percent of that day and in those circumstances is or is not my 100 percent real potentiality. By opposition, I lose when I don't give my 100 percent.

For example, in the saddest moment of my life I felt that I could not concentrate, that my head was not working. In those moments giving everything meant getting out of bed, bathing, getting dressed, and doing the minimum of work. This is to value yourself, respect yourself and understand the limits. It is being compassionate with yourself, and understanding that there are things that time fixes, being patient is key. And it passes, the sadness passes.

The session ended with Mr. E excited, going to play the tournament that he had that afternoon, with the conviction that he was going to win, even though he consciously knew that this time he had not set himself up for success with such anticipation.

When we set ourselves up for success, we prepare ourselves physically and mentally for the activity we are going to do. That is, in the case of a tennis tournament, the night before we eat and drink accordingly, we rest long enough, we hydrate well, we warm up, and we give our 100 percent with the conviction that we are winners.

Can we tell the difference in the result?

When we overthink certain decisions, they affect the resources and the result. On the other hand, when we have a system that allows us to simplify the decision-making process, we have a better predisposition, and we make better use of resources, in this way, we enjoy it regardless of the result.

When we talk about purpose, these concepts are important because they have a positive or negative connotation in our state of mind, that is why I invite you to live with joy and enjoy every moment on purpose!

Another hold back for me has been self-sabotage:

The feeling of not giving my 100 percent, the need for external validation, the fact that I was betraying my instinct and what I liked, all those limiting beliefs and thoughts that I used to tell about myself. I didn't struggle to build healthy and productive habits, but I wasn't giving my 100 percent on them.

For me it was just the thought that I wasn't good enough, and the fear of becoming arrogant, I was confusing humbleness with acknowledging when I've done something well. It was also the fact that as women we normally don't have a healthy relationship with some concepts such as success and ambition.

The importance of changing the mindset lies in turning weaknesses into strengths, accepting out of normal as special and extraordinary, avoiding thoughts that would limit ourselves and prevent us from reaching our full potential.

I used to think that "Things were harder for me than for other people" and for that reason, things were harder for me! I was already calling it, I was manifesting against myself, and also it had to do with me self-sabotaging: I used to get distracted after some time while I was sitting for an exam. Eventually I noticed that, and the pattern was that I was getting distracted as soon as I felt I would pass it. So for some time I would study a lot and I wouldn't get high marks, unconsciously this was aligned with the limiting belief that "everything was harder for me than for other people."

When I noticed that, I decided to change it. So I recognized the feeling with a picture: Do you know when you grab some sand on the beach, and it starts to fall from your hand. But then, you press it harder and it stops falling?

Well, that was my empowerment. Every time I was sitting at an exam, at some point I would make the decision of pressing my hand harder. I was determined not to let the sand slip from my hand. And guess what? Yes, I started getting higher grades!

There are many times of betraying ourselves, the last time I recall betraying my intuitive self was when I was going with my brothers and sisters to a festival. At that point in my life I already knew that those were not for me, I didn't enjoy them, and I had said "no" to many of them. But this time I said "yes, I will go" because I didn't want to miss the opportunity of sharing the moment with them.

Somehow I felt in my gut that I shouldn't go. While we were there, I wasn't enjoying the festival itself, but I was having a good time with my siblings. At some point someone talked to me for a moment, and two minutes later, the person disappeared, and my phone was gone from my purse also.

That was the last day, that was the day I promised myself I would only go where I wanted to go, and I worked to get deeply connected and respect my instinct.

I understand that we learn to be more rational and to make decisions mostly through our brain or our heart. But there's another way also, our gut, our instinct. I am sure we all felt it many times, in different situations, we had that feeling that we can't explain, and for no reason we choose to ignore it.

In my experience, I learned to be connected with my instinct in my professional life, not that much in my personal life.

Through working with people I learned patterns, and to make decisions not only based on facts, and hardly ever based on my heart, even though I consider myself a human and compassionate leader, but instead, I go with my gut.

In my personal life, I used to think that I had to enjoy what "normal people" would enjoy, so I used to push myself to go out, or do some activities, just because they were supposed to be fun. And to be honest, I was having a great time, but it had to do more with the activities I wasn't doing such as dancing, or singing, or going out to a place I wanted to go. How watching a movie would seem boring, while for me it was fun. I would enjoy relaxing and have a quiet night, but instead I was pushing myself to do what others preferred to do. Again, I was enjoying going out, it's just that some-times it wasn't my favorite option for a plan.

It was a game changer for me to discover and accept what I wanted and liked to do.

This hold back has to do with being a perfectionist also. Did you know that one of the most productive cultures in the world has to do with the fact that the only perfect is God, so they leave a defect on each item? [I need to find a source for this]

Perfectionism is one of the biggest reasons why people don't move forward, it has to do with the feeling of never being ready, of not knowing enough, but at the end of the day there are only so many things that we know, and if we have to wait until we are ready, we will never be.

One of the first acknowledgements I had with the process of writing this book was that I needed to feel ready from my heart and my gut, but my head will never be ready, and when I started to list all the ideas, it was a never-ending process. Thank God for my coach that pushed me to start writing and came to the agreement that I would go back to review the chapters later. At that point we discussed that there are only some ideas that you can include in a book, there's not a thing such as a "complete" book, so starting from that understanding, it was easier to move forward.

As I told you before, I recall that there was a moment when I was at university that I made the decision to break that pattern and I decided to empower myself and go for everything and more. It was an internal process, as well as a mental one. It has to do with listening to that little voice inside you saying that you can, and you will, that you are unstoppable, and that no matter what, you will make it happen.

Yesterday I was talking with someone, and at some point he said, "I have defects" and I asked him how he could say that in a different way. At the beginning he avoided the question because it was uncomfortable, but I asked him again, and it was hard for him to express that with a positive connotation, especially because he was saying that entrepreneurs evaluate themselves on a daily basis and that they have defects.

Being honest, I check in with myself many times a day. However, I don't evaluate my performance and development on a daily basis. I understand that it was a measurement of the yardstick he is using to measure himself. Anyway, my opinion in this matter is that part of having an intention and living according to our own rules is to understand that words have weight, and the deeper awareness we have on our expressions, the better we will send the messages to ourselves, then we will act accordingly.

Let's paraphrase this example: "I have defects," in a

context of development and continuous improvement, it's not "I am a human I have defects as we all have."

So here are some options:

"As an entrepreneur, every day is an opportunity to face a new challenge/improvement/lesson to learn"

This way we are accepting that we may go through some hard times, and at the same time we are facing them with positivity and the certainty that we will learn and get through it.

Comparisons. What a topic!

As we discussed before, not even identical twins are identical, then, Why do we compare ourselves to other people?

We are all different, and that's why different things mean different challenges or difficulties for each of us. We normally don't go around talking to other people mentioning those issues, so what other people see is through their own filters.

It was a huge challenge for me to post reels and videos on Instagram, but it seems that I needed to get that done, so I made a plan, I would do one video a week. Over a couple of weeks I was already doing them faster, with more confidence and natural. I am fine with my accent, it's just that when I get nervous the words don't come to me.

I was in one session with a coachee who a coach is too, and we are working on his own practice, so he told me that when he sees my videos speaking English he gets anxious and freaks out. That day I realized that we never see the whole picture, not only on social media, but in life. We only know a little bit about other people's struggles so we should just assume that they have their struggles and we don't know about them, and avoid comparisons at all cost, especially when they are not motivating us. Comparisons can be used as motivation, I get that. However, if it's not bringing anything positive, then avoid that kind of thought.

And this leads me to "Anxiety."

Anxiety is coming from worrying about future situations today. We already had this conversation, there's no point in worrying, just make a short plan, focus on the next steps, and trust the journey. Avoid thinking about those challenges that may come later and trust that you will have all the tools and resources you will need to move forward.

When I started my coaching practice, I made sure to face only a limited amount of challenges at a time, and trust me, I pushed myself, but respecting my limits was a key to be able to keep on moving forward consistently and avoid burnt outs.

This also has to do with being scared of failing. All those "What if?" that we have in our heads. What is the problem with failing? I will tell you, failing has only one problem and it is if we didn't learn anything. Other than that, failures are what took people to high places, so first of all, being scared of things that didn't happen yet it's just a waste of time and energy. I am not saying that we shouldn't consider all the options, and deltas, and possibilities. But what we need to accept is that even if we analyze 100 scenarios with different variables, there are at least another 1000 that are out of our control and may produce a turn in events, so to think that we can start a project without any risk is absurd. Life is a risk itself!

My suggestion for this one is to make a list of those "what if?" until we come to the point where the ultimate consequence or risk is just nothing.

In my personal opinion, I'd rather deal with the consequences than wondering what could have happened if I took that other road. I am the kind of person that once a possibility door is open, I can't go back, I need to go through it. I couldn't live with the regret of what was left undone.

JOURNAL IT

16

YOUR OWN RULES!

It all comes to an end; this book is getting there also.

Through the sections we've been collecting tools, methods, perspective, and hopefully new ideas.

We started this journey with an equation, and we went over it. We explored our gifts, we learned how to create new passions, we reflected on our values and the importance of being clear about them, we learned how to set goals and then make a plan to accomplish them, and by the end, we went over the importance of aligning all those parts of the equation to find our purpose and live according to it.

If I had to point out the most important topic that I chose to include in the book, I would choose self-love. This whole book comes down to it, to love yourself as you love others. Treat yourself as you treat your best friends, because they are still people, they are not perfect, they are not flawless, but you love, accept, respect, and admire them. They do have limiting and old beliefs, but you don't know them, and if you do, you help them to change their perspective, so why wouldn't you do that with yourself?

Through loving yourself, you will love others, and though

loving others, you will love yourself more, it is a growing cycle. Be the best friend you would like to have, and be that person for yourself, because nobody deserves your love more than you do. You are enough, you are more than enough, you are extraordinary, and every single part of you deserves to be embraced.

I've been thinking about all those normal behaviors we have towards others, that are not intentionally loving, so I'd like to talk about some of those that would help us be the person the world deserves, and specially, the person that we can become, and we deserve.

Let's normalize to treat each other well, to accept, look and see each other without judging, just finding the positive. Let's normalize to listen to each other and ask from genuine curiosity, from interest of knowing how the other person is doing or what is needed. Let's normalize laughing with each other. Let's stop justifying people for bad behaviors. Let's normalize treating each other with love and being more empathic. Let's normalize accepting other people's decisions without giving an opinion, especially if we disagree, let's just limit ourselves to mention our concern or doubts that we have, but not trying to make the other person change the plan just because we don't feel that is a good idea.

Let's normalize learning before talking about something, there's a difference between an opinion and feedback. I see so many posts on Instagram explaining important topics from ignorance and aggressiveness that it doesn't even make sense. Let's respect each other's ideas and understand that we are all advocates for different causes that are important to create an impact and live in a better world. I can't talk about the impact that eating meat or buying in big clothing brands is creating in the environment, but I can listen to the people that know and make decisions that get me closer to the ideal, so I can add my grain of sand. After reading about racism and inequality, I think that it is a topic that we need to discuss. Something that it's terrible for me is that, according to Dr. Nicole LePera, racism and inequality affects people's behaviors and body responses in a permanent way. So, when discussing these topics, do you think that it is all reduced to "treating everyone in the same way"? Well, not! To make sure that we are making changes we need to inform and educate ourselves, and instead of discussing or refuting, just listen to people that have more knowledge, even if it is just a little more.

Let's stop normalizing that some kind of education, university or career is giving more validation or weight to our words. Let's stop normalizing that we all have different worth according to ridiculous yardsticks such as body shape, money, gender, sexual preferences, race, nationality, or followers on Instagram.

Let's normalize real beauty, the one that comes from within, goodness, kindness, love.

Let's stop normalizing excuses, because they are useful only for those who have the privilege of being up to social standards and feel comfortable in that position.

Let's normalize making other people uncomfortable by discussing all these matters, to speak up when we disagree, and I know that it is not easy, sometimes I get tired of defending my perspective on these topics, but I keep on reading and educating myself, so I have more knowledge and better reasoning.

As I said before, it all comes down to self-love, because if we put out great energy, that's what we will get back, even if it sounds selfish, it's not, it all starts from you, and for you to show up for others at your best, you need to start by loving yourself. Also, because through self-love is that we will make thoughtful and intentional choices, and that's how we will live through our purpose.

It was my intention for you to find the wakeup call you are looking for, to find the questions and the safe space to answer. The guide to start moving forward through a shift in the mindset and the development of new habits. The opportunity to train your mind and become a person that sets herself up for success. The redefinition of many words that we normally use, and we don't consider the weight they have, and then, the understanding of the fact that words have weight, we can't go around just saying whatever crosses our mind. The acknowledgement of the importance of considering different points of view and that the change in perspective depends on us. The training to become more conscious and the choice of living intentionally. The transformative path that ends on owning our own truth and becoming responsible for the decisions we make and facing the consequences those have.

I wrote this book with a mix of personal and professional experiences because for me the purpose can be found in different ways and areas of our lives.

Also, because we have only twenty-four hours a day and if we spend eight hours being miserable and frustrated in a job position that is giving us nothing but stress, just know that you can change that, it is an option, because there are always options.

I shared some personal challenges and pressures that I felt, hoping that you connect and know that you are not alone, I am here, and I get you!

We need to learn how to reroute the brain to have the opportunities that we are not seeing. Yes, to make those changes requires taking some risks, but isn't it just life? What would life be without any risk? I am not saying that we need to live as if we didn't care about anything, I am saying that we need to control what we can control and take impactful and massive action that will take us where we want to be, tomorrow, in six months, maybe in two years, but if you never start, you will never get there.

It is important that you don't get trapped between your passions and your purpose, just remember that your purpose is your light, it is the whole picture, it has to do with your legacy, with the way you would like to transcend and to be remembered, is that priceless experience that brings you joy, fulfilment and sets the yardstick that rules your life and makes you choose consistently.

In the end, the purpose for me is love, and mine is to live in a better world, where there is more kindness, opportunities, and equality for all. I am trying to do my part by creating an impact on the leaders, because real leaders create more leaders, and each of us is a leader!

To find a purpose is the alignment of your whole self. It is getting rid at your own peace of all the inconsistencies in your life. It is freedom!

What do you think freedom is? How does freedom look like for you?

For me, to be free is to do what I want, when I want and how I want it, acknowledging that nobody will do it in the same way I will, just because I am extraordinary. This means that I am happy and grateful for being able to do whatever I do, despite the result.

Through this acknowledgement, I am also at peace with the fact that I am not perfect, and that not everyone has to like me. The most important relationship I have in my life is with myself, and for many years I haven't taken care of it properly, and it's a pity because I am my best company.

I am committed to keeping this love alive, since it is the light and power of all the other loves. To love yourself is to love the people around you. And to love yourself is to prioritize and respect your whole person, mind, heart, body, and soul.

Take your time, just remember that life will keep on happening, whether you are active or passive about it, and the sooner you get in charge and take responsibility for your decisions the better.

Remember, the difference between what could have happened and what actually happened was that single moment when you made the decision, was that leap of faith that you took or that you didn't, was that door that you decided to cross or you chose to close, and once you made that decision, it can't be done what was undone and vice versa. I'd rather regret what I did than keep saying "What if?" in my mind. What would you choose the next time you have the opportunity to make history, your own history!

And what is more, there are just a few things that I regret, but even those things taught me something. What I can't do is learn the lessons that I didn't experience, so I'd rather learn, I'd rather fall, I'd rather be broken, and then stand up, and slowly start to move forward again.

We all need to be broken, to grow, to learn, to evolve. A seed needs to be broken to create new life and grow, and we aren't different.

There's a reason why I did not know all these things before, and that is because I had to be broken. We are all broken at some point, and through that place is where light gets in, that way you can go deep inside your soul. Healing comes from being broken.

I started this book because I wanted to share with other people all those lessons that life had been giving me the past years, it seems that I even did it a little unconsciously.

What I didn't expect was for this book to be a milestone in my healing path. Through this book I had the opportunity to go deeper in my heart and soul through those broken spaces and I found myself, I found so much love, so many new perspectives, I found that all my history makes sense, that God and the universe brought me here and nothing in the path wasn't aligned with my ultimate purpose, love.

I hope that you enjoyed the reading, that you found a lot of questions and some answers, that you have many new ideas and strategies to try, that you feel the encouragement to be in charge!

I wish you brave and impactful decisions, humbleness to accept what we can't change, faith to surrender and receive what is meant to be for you and the courage to live your life by your own rules!!

JOURNAL IT

ACKNOWLEDGMENTS

I believe that people and events come to our life to leave a lesson. Some people, soulmates, are forever tutors, those that came to your life and will be there "forever". Some others will come and go, and I always feel lucky to have the opportunity to learn from each person and each experience, even if it's a very short moment.

For this reason I want to thank every person who has been part of this journey, this book belongs to each of you.

Haydee and Jose, my parents, for never giving up, for teaching us to go for everything and more, for being supportive even when our decisions were hard for them. For believing in me. To my mother, for seeing me. To my father, for encouraging me.

Maxi, Fiore, Baru and Juan, my siblings, soulmates and forever tutors. For being there, for becoming this team that no matter what will be together. For the support, for the love. Because together we are stronger. Maxi for your humbleness, for opening up and being part of this experience. Fiore, for embracing me, for being my home when I didn't know where my home was, for your support. Baru, for your freedom, for your encouragement to be my best version, for your light, for all those little details that make me feel seen and loved. Juan, for sharing all the writing experience with me, for being an infinite source of inspiration and light, for being an example on how to be a warrior, for opening paths.

To my female ancestors, for being an example of evolution, integrity, independence, for being examples of how to be the hearts of each family, for encouraging me to be myself, for their pride and support in my journey.

Andrae Smith Jr., my writing coach and editor, I will be forever grateful for having the opportunity to go through this journey with you, this wouldn't have been possible without your compassion, commitment, and patience.

Valentina Lava, I am honored to have you in my team, and specially to be part of your family. I am beyond grateful for your support on every step and every level, as a sister-in-law, and as a professional. For your love, patience, and encouragement. I am looking forward to keeping on facing challenges together!

Mariano, my brother-in-law, for being family, for your love, generosity, and care.

My soul-sisters, Laurita and Malu. For being there for me, unconditionally, sharing the highs and the lows. Laurita, my thinking partner, the eldest sister that life gave me. Malu, my BFF, because life is better with friends that become family like you. Because I feel normal around both of you. Let's keep on being "special" together!

Cathy, the friend that the universe sent me. My craziest friend. Thank you for helping me navigate this year, for your love, compassion, and amazing energy! For always laughing at difficulties and making the most out of every moment.

To my therapist, Justo. Because he's been unconditional through the hardest moments, most of my lessons come from our sessions, for partnering with me in my commitment to my wellbeing. For your support, encouragement, and trust.

To all the accountability and thinking partners that I had along the way, you know who you are.

To you, because through reading this book, you've become part of its journey!